Rent Utilization in China's Auto Industry

中国汽车产业中的租金利用研究

高建奕 / 著

知识产权出版社
全国百佳图书出版单位

图书在版编目（CIP）数据

中国汽车产业中的租金利用研究 = Rent Utilization in China's Auto Industry：英文/高建奕著．—北京：知识产权出版社，2019.7

ISBN 978-7-5130-6344-9

Ⅰ．①中…　Ⅱ．①高…　Ⅲ．①汽车工业—租金—利用—研究—中国—英文
Ⅳ．①F426.471

中国版本图书馆 CIP 数据核字（2019）第 126115 号

内容简介

本书的研究将传统的寻租概念拓展为包含租金创造、租金分配和租金寻求三个相互联系而又分开的过程的租金利用模型，并以此来分析中国汽车产业发展过程中的租金及寻租现象。研究发现作为"计划经济活化石"的汽车产业自诞生之日起长期受到政府严格控制，租金和寻租现象大量存在。从一定意义上说，以计划为基础的经济本身是个庞大但不精巧的租金利用机器，租金的创造、分配和寻求是内嵌于中国的整个汽车产业管理体制中的，而寻租活动在带来大量社会资源浪费的同时客观上成了推动汽车行业"市场化"的力量。本研究从理论上看拓展了传统寻租理论的解释力，特别是对长期存在计划因素的我国经济发展中寻租现象的解释；从实践方面看，对于厘清我国经济发展中寻租与产业发展之间的关系有所助益。

策划编辑：杨晓红　　**责任校对**：谷　洋
责任编辑：兰　涛　　**责任印制**：孙婷婷
封面设计：郑　重

中国汽车产业中的租金利用研究

Rent Utilization in China's Auto Industry

高建奕　著

出版发行：知识产权出版社有限责任公司　　**网　址**：http：//www.ipph.cn
社　址：北京市海淀区气象路 50 号院　　**邮　编**：100081
责编电话：010-82000860 转 8325　　**责编邮箱**：lantao@cnipr.com
发行电话：010-82000860 转 8101/8102　　**发行传真**：010-82000893/82005070/82000270
印　刷：北京虎彩文化传播有限公司　　**经　销**：各大网上书店、新华书店及相关专业书店
开　本：720mm × 1000mm　1/16　　**印　张**：10.5
版　次：2019 年 7 月第 1 版　　**印　次**：2019 年 7 月第 1 次印刷
字　数：180 千字　　**定　价**：48.00 元

ISBN 978-7-5130-6344-9

鸣　谢

本书的出版得到了平顶山学院博士科研启动基金课题（PXY-BSQD-2018032）的支持，特此致谢！

Special Acknowledgement

The publication of this book is funded by Doctoral Research Start-up Fund of Pingdingshan University (PXY-BSQD-2018032).

Preface

When mentioning rent seeking, conventional wisdom believes that rent seeking is nothing but a pathological phenomenon because rent seeking constitutes a type of unproductive activity which results in social loss and is thus growth-retarding. Recent study, however, shows a different story. It is said that rents are ubiquitous and of different types; rents are able to be created and allocated in many ways; rent seeking has complicated and profound implications to economic growth.

Rather than conventional rent-seeking approach from methodological individualism, this book applies a much more far-reaching approach from an institutional perspective. Following the approach advanced by Boyd and Ngo among many others, this book puts forward an analytical model of "rent-utilization" and identifies it into three phases, i.e. rent creation, rent allocation and rent-seeking, extending the application of classical rent-seeking approach towards China's auto industry in a plan-based economic system.

The central purpose of this book is to discuss the rent utilization in China's auto industry, to explain how it shapes, if not totally, at least partly, the development of the auto industry, focusing on the types of rents, and on the actors, both individual and institutional, and on the related outcomes, both the economic and political, and on the influential factors, both formally and informally institutional, in the different development stages.

China's auto industry has experienced over 60-year development since the early 1950s, which is roughly divided into two halves in this book. The first half (the mid-1950s through 1978) in the centrally planned economy is termed as "Before Reform" stage, and the second half (1979 through the mid-2000s) in the transitional economy as "After Reform" stage.

The study in this book showed some findings conflicting with existing conclusions. The mainstream literature denies that the existence of rent-seeking activities, even the existence of rents, in the centrally planned economy, but this study found that institutional rent created by central government through price control was the main sources of rent before Reform, and this type of rent endogenously originated from the planned economic system per se and lasted for a long time.

Rent-seeking activities appeared along the whole development process of China's auto industry, whether before or after the Reform. Rent-seeking by local governments was a common phenomenon in both stages. The sharp difference between before Reform and after Reform was that the enterprises, especially the State-Owned Enterprises (SOEs) that gained some autonomy from the governments became another main actor of rent-seeking with many means. Besides, non-state owned enterprises, such as foreign enterprises and private enterprises also began to enter the rent-seeking game after Reform.

Rent-seeking per se in China's auto industry could be identified as a means of destroying the monopoly of the state. In the plan-based economy, the state taking the central government as its first-level agent was the unique legitimate owner of all the rents. The central government attempted to strengthen its authority by re-centralization but failed every time. Although the ostensible target of rent-seeking by local governments and enterprises was the rents of all types created by the state, what they really attempted to change was the institutional arrangements inside the multilayered and fragmented structure of rent allocation. In other words, centrally tight control was impossible without the change of that existed multilayered and fragmented structure. Therefore, the widespread rent-seeking activities by local governments conspired with enterprises could be considered as one of the critical factors that push the market-oriented reform to come true.

In the plan-based economy, the state was an elaborate but imperfect device of rent utilization. The central government created substantial rents to develop the auto industry as one of pillar industries. It established corresponding institutional arrangements in order to attain the goal of this industrial policy. As the monopolistic owner of these rents, it allocated them to local governments with multi-levels of hierarchies and to some SOEs. In the process, substantial autonomy with oversight authority was transferred to local governments.The M-form hierarchical structure, formal decentralizations, information asymmetry and geographical remoteness caused the relationship between central and local governments to form multiple principal-agent situations. Thus, a structure of rent utilization for the auto industry was fragmented in the central government agencies and multi-layered among the central-local governments from the day of its birth. The administrative decentralization that transferred authority from the central to local governments before and after Reform strengthened this multi-layered nature while the economic decentralization that transferred authority from governments to enterprises and families made the whole structure more fragmented and divided, and finally the resultant force of them ended it in the early 2000s.

In other words, the rent utilization was embedded in the regulatory framework which governs industrial and economic developments at the national level as well as the local level. To a great extent, rent utilization in China was institutionalized as the constitutive part of economic governance through intimately connecting to the political system.

Rent-seeking in plan-based economies has been out of research focus area for a long time. The model of rent-utilization in this book does not reject or deny the wisdom of classical rent-seeking theory. Rather, this model complements and supports it.

This book is a revised and updated version of my doctoral dissertation *Rent Utilization in a Plan-based Economy: Extension of Rent-seeking Theory towards China's Auto Industry*. I would like to express my sincere gratitude to the following people among many others who supported me during the writing of my doctoral dissertation and the publication of this book.

To my supervisor, Professor Kim Haengbum, for his friendly encouragement, his academic rigor and his patient guidance in supervisions, for his tolerance in personality, and his fatherly selfless help in my everyday life. Honestly, my doctoral dissertation could not have been completed and this book could not have been published without Professor Kim's assistance and guidance.

To the Committee Members for my doctoral dissertation, Professor Kang Yunho, Professor Park Minjeong, Profesor Kim Insin, especially the Chair, Professor Hahn Inkeun, who read the text for several times and gave me specific advice, for their constructive suggestions.

To the two anonymous referees and Professor Lee Seong-gyu for their professional suggestions on the early version of my doctoral dissertation.

To Professor Kang, Professor Park, and Assistant Lee, and all the other professors in Public Administration Department of Pusan National University, for their sincerely help.

To my colleagues both at International College of the University of Suwon and School of Political Science and Law of Pingdingshan University for their friendly help.

To Ms. Yang Xiaohong, the Deputy Director, and Ms. Lantao, the Copyeditor both from Intellectual Property Publishing House Co., Ltd. for their patient help and professional service. If there are any errors, they are not theirs, but all mine.

Finally I would like to thank all my family for their love and support. Thank my dear wife, Zhang Shu, who has been and will always go to the end of the world together with me, for her sincere trust, her affectionate companionship, her pure love and her sacrifice for our family. Thank my lovely daughter, Gao Shalang(Sharon), for the supreme surprise and joy she has brought to me. Sharon is an angel and a mascot, whom God sent to me in the middle of my second and third round dissertation defense to let me accomplish my "mission" — A doctoral candidate has to pass at least three round dissertation defenses before earning a Ph.D. in Pusan National University. Her lovely face, and even her occasional cry brought me great pleasure to my nervons writing life.

I would like to express my heartfelt thanks to my Parents-in-law, Zhang Fang and Shu Yulan, for their tolerance and confidence in me, for their painstaking care for all of us.

I owe a real debt to my parents, Gao Zhenyun and Zhang Guifang, who now live in the heaven without pain and worry, for their endless love and selfless support. Without them, I could not have come so far in my life. I owed them so much that I could not pay them back forever. I hope that I could meet them again and be reborn as their son in the heaven. I dedicate this book to my parents.

Gao Jianyi

March 4th, 2019

Contents

List of Tables

List of Figures

Ⅰ. Introduction

1.1 Purpose

Although rent seeking has been a hot research topic in social science, such as Economics, Politics and Public Administration since around the mid-1970s, most literature on it is focused on market-based economies, and few is founded on plan-based economies. Initially, the rent-seeking theory is closely related to monopoly under market-based economies.[①] All the rent-seeking studies of Virginian mainstream such as Tullock, Rowley, Tollison, Congleton etc. follow this tradition while most empirical studies pay attention to rent seeking in market-based economies, focusing on the interaction

① Just as Krueger (1974), the creator of the term "rent seeking", states in the beginning part in her essay, "In many market-oriented economies, government restrictions upon economic activity are pervasive facts of life. These restrictions give rise to rents in a variety of forms, and people often compete for the rents. Sometimes such competition is perfectly legal. In other instances, rent seeking takes other forms, such as bribery, corruption, smuggling and black markets."

between "private sector" and "government" .[①]

Then does it mean that non-market economic system is so healthy that it has no relation to rent-seeking phenomena? The answer is No. In fact, rent is created and rent-seeking is ubiquitous in every economy, whether market-oriented or plan-based. Rent and rent-seeking are twined with government intervention, and where there is regulation whether by capitalism or socialism, there is rent and rent-seeking. However, just as Boyd (2009:255) says, the rent-seeking theory of Public Choice theorists is characterized by a (political) market-rent nexus focusing almost exclusively on the United States of America. Therefore, it is of great importance to identify aspects of rent seeking in a plan-based economy where regulation *per se* is raison d'être of government from a much broader respective.

China had been a plan-based economy from the mid-1950s to the early 2000s when China proclaimed its accession to WTO. China was under the centrally planned economic system roughly since the mid-1950s short after maintaining a market-based economy for a short time.[②] Throughout the following 20 years, China's economy zigzagged along the two waves of administrative decentralization and deviated

① See Boyd's empirical studies of Mexico, Japan and China Taiwan (Boyd, 2005, 2006); Khan and Jomo (2000) studied on south eastern Asian countries; Yoon's (1991) research on rent seeking in the process of economic growth in Korea, and many others.

② China had maintained a market-based economy by roughly the mid-1950s after its foundation in 1949 under the guidance of New Democracy (Hu, 2008:108~121).

gradually from the orthodox centrally planned economic system. Since the "Reform" (1978), China has gradually stepped out of the centrally planned economy and a market-oriented economy started to develop. Experiencing a hybrid economy under which the traditional central planning and the emerging market system coexisted as means of resource allocation during the whole 1980s, it finally adopted a so-called "socialism market economy" in the mid-1990s. With the reform moving on, China's market-based economy obtained an international recognition after accession to WTO at the end of 2001.

However, most studies on rent seeking in China focus on the after Reform stage when a market-oriented reform was under way. In fact, the initial purpose of introducing rent-seeking theory into China was to explain the serious corruption emerged in the process of market-oriented reform.[①] Quite a few scholars deny the existence of rent-seeking activities, even the existence of rents, in the centrally planned economy, while they argue that

---

① Wu Jinglian, a famous economist in China, introduced the rent seeking theory on the academic journal called "Comparative Economic and Social System" (Wu was the editor of it then) two years after Buchanan received the Nobel Prize in economics in 1986. Most of them are introductions or interpretations of the theory. Many of the famous papers on rent seeking, such as Krueger's "the political economics of rent seeking society" (Comparative Economic and Social System, No.5, 1988), and Buchanan's "rent seeking and profit seeking" (Comparative Economic and Social System, No.6, 1988), was printed in Chinese version. Some are engaged in estimating the costs of rent-seeking activities under the Chinese transition economy, and much more try to explain the corruption phenomenon prevailing in reality.

rent-seeking activities by local governments and state-owned enterprises were widespread in economic development after Reform.

However, some other scholars, including Fung (1987), Hu Xiaobo (2009), Lin et al. (2003) and Wedeman (2003) argue that substantial rents had already existed in the centrally planned economy before Reform. However, they did not hold the same view on whether there were rent-seeking activities under the centrally planned economic system on the one hand, and on the other hand, all scholars just theoretically analyzed rent-seeking in the centrally planned economy, failing to provide empirical studies based on historical fact.

This causes a series of questions: were substantial rents actually created in the plan-based economy, especially in the centrally planned economy? If so, in what form and by what means were they created? How were the rents allocated? Did the rent-seeking activities exist? If it existed, who were the rent-seekers? Were the state-owned enterprises the main rent-seekers as they had been in the era of after Reform era? What about the local governments? What effect did the rent-seeking activities exert on the country's industrial development?

This study is to identify the aspects of rent-seeking in China's economy which went through the plan-based economy. The primary purpose is to find out whether there were rents and rent-seeking activities in the development process of China's auto industry in the plan-based economy, especially the centrally planned economic context. The central purpose is to find out what roles the central government, local governments, and enterprises play in the whole development process of China's auto industry in the plan-based economic context with a broader analytical model of rent utilization.①

The auto industry was chosen as the object of analysis for the following reasons. Firstly, the auto industry had been under heavy-handed control by the state from the very beginning until recently, famous for a "living fossil" of planned economy in China. Secondly, the auto industry is one of the important "pillar industries" in China, so it could represent the development of similar sectors and even the whole national economy. By so doing, this would contribute to complete understanding how the rent utilization in the plan-based economic context shaped the development of China's auto industry. This would also help to understand how rent seeking activities in a plan-based economy are different from those in the market-based economy. This would contribute to extending the validity of rent-seeking theory.

1.2 Object and Scope

The automobile is regarded as "the machine that changed the world"②, and the auto industry is considered as "the industry of industries". As Chong Chu-young (2004:118), the founder of Hyundai Group and the father of

① See the Model of Rent Utilization in part two of chapter. Ⅱ of this book.

② This is the title of a classic book written by James P. Womack, Daniel T. Jones and Daniel Roos (2007). In the book, they focus on the evolution of the lean production in the auto industry originated from Toyota.

South Korea's auto industry, put it in his memoir, the auto industry is so important in the economic development of a country that it can be viewed as the economic indicator of the country. It is one of the capital-incentive and technology-incentive industries handling about 30,000 parts, and it is linked to many other industrial sectors and thus it even dominates the whole industrial development of a country. Therefore, the auto industry is traditionally a central pillar of the manufacturing economies of many developed countries including Germany, France, the United States and Japan, and the latecomer South Korea. Although it should be a highly competing industry, the development of auto industry often sees government intervention to a greater or lesser extent. The government intervention is less in the case of the United States but it is more in some other countries such as Japan and South Korea. Government intervention in both Japan and South Korea shares the same hypothesis: to eliminate excessive competition, to prevent duplication of production, and to achieve economies of scale (Ngo & Chen, 2009). The government sets up related industrial policies and uses different policy instruments such as market closure, tax relief and subsidies and so on. The selected automakers are offered various forms of supports and privileges. As such, the development of auto industry in these countries has been intimately connected with the process of the creation, allocation, and pursuit of different kinds of rents and rent-like transfers. Therefore, the auto industry is a good case to study rent utilization.

Ⅰ. Introduction

The Chinese auto industry has experienced an about 60-year development since the early 1950s, which can be roughly divided into two stages. The dividing line is the end of 1978 when a market-oriented reform started. The first stage started from the early 1950s to the late 1970s, and the second from the early 1980s up to now. However, China's market-based economy obtained an international recognition and the substantial "liberalization" of auto industry realized to some extent after accession to WTO in the end of 2001. Therefore, this study confines the time span to the period from the mid-1950s to the mid-2000s. The first stage (the mid-1950s through 1978) in the centrally planned economy is termed as "Before Reform" stage, and the second half (namely, 1979 through the mid-2000s) in the transitional economy as "After Reform" stage.

During the "Before Reform" stage, its whole development, from planning to production to distribution, was under the control of governments rather than a market mechanism. There was no particular industrial policy made for the auto industry. As one of the most important heavy industrial sectors, auto industry benefited from the price-distorted macro-policy for the capital formation of the whole heavy industry, but as a whole, it developed in a zigzag with low production capability, fragmented structure, and backward technology in a relatively closed context under the planned economic system.

At the beginning of the "After Reform" stage, China began to redevelop its auto industry, especially the passenger car sector in the context of the market-orientation reform characterized by a hybrid economic system under which traditional central planning and the emerging market coexisted as means of resource allocation. The auto industry was chosen as one of the pillar industry after the haphazard growth in the first half of the 1980s. Then the "Large Three and Little Three" strategy and the 1994 Auto Industrial Policy were made and implemented in succession. Under the heavy-handed government intervention, the auto industry proliferated fast in the 1990s. High rents were created in the industry and invited extensive rent-seeking activities. With some more in-depth reform in the mid-1990s, Chinese government gradually lowered the import tariff for finished cars and deregulated the state fixed prices for motor vehicles and the entry restriction. After China's accession to the WTO in the end of 2001, which means that market economy in China had obtained recognition by the international society and the traditional plan-based economic system had faded out, almost all the famous transnational automakers entered into China and built their joint ventures. Some homegrown auto enterprises with their own independent car models also obtained the approval to produce passenger cars. Bitter price wars broke out frequently, the persistently higher-priced passenger cars dramatically reduced, and the high rents in the auto industry, especially in the passenger car sector dissipated gradually.

Rare studies among a large body of literature on China's auto industrial development[①] directly focus on rent seeking activities. Huang (2003) analyzes how China failed to allocate rents efficiently due to the divided and fragmented institutional arrangement. Yu (2005) analyzes the reason for the failure of Chinese auto industrial policy after Reform from the perspective of rent-seeking in the narrow sense. Wu (2010) discusses the roles of local governments in the process of rent-seeking and the effects on the industry development through case studies on beer and auto industries. Wedeman (2009) discusses the impact of rents and rent-seeking in the mergers and acquisitions on local protectionism through case study on auto and beer industries. Ngo & Chen (2009) discuss how the rent production affects the emergence and a subsequent decline of the oligopolistic structure of China's auto industry after Reform. Chen (2010) analyzes the reason for the rise of domestic brand auto enterprises in China from the rent-seeking perspective.

Comprehensively evaluating these studies, we can find that all of them focus on China's auto development after Reform (1978) firstly. Secondly, all there studies focus merely on a singular aspect, and there is no overall study of the auto industry. Thirdly, almost all the studies focus on rent exchange in a single term of rent-seeking. In order to make up these deficiencies, this study will extend the time frame to the development process of China's

① The most comprehensive studies on the development of China's auto industrial development come from Harwit (1995), Thun (2006), and Chin (2010).

auto industry in the plan-based economy and discuss all the aspects from a broader perspective of rent utilization. However, the period from mid-2000s when the "liberalization" of the auto industry was realized to some extent will not be included in this study.

1.3 Methodology

This study is to discuss the aspects of rent utilization in China's plan-based economic context. In order to realize this purpose, this study applies several methods as follows.

Firstly, this study applies qualitative method rather than quantitative one. Instead of estimating the welfare losses from rent-seeking, the primary purpose of this study is to identify whether the rents and rent-seeking activities exist in China's auto industry under the plan-based economic system, especially under the centrally planned economic system. In other words, this study focuses on how rents are created, allocated and sought in the development process of China's auto industry. In China's economic and political context, industrial development is often closely related to political and institutional factors. Therefore, a qualitative approach is much more appropriate than a quantitative one.

Secondly, this study applies case study focusing on empirical data rather than theoretical explanation. The auto industry is used as the case to discuss rent utilization in China's plan-based economic context.

Thirdly, this study is a diachronic comparison study. According to the macro institutional differences, this study divides the evolution of China's auto industry into two different stages and makes a diachronic comparison between these two stages on three aspects of rent utilization.

Ⅱ . Theoretical Background and Analytical Framework

2.1 Rent-seeking Theory

This study is to analyze what roles the governments, central and local, and enterprises of all kinds play in the China's auto industrial development in the plan-based economy from a broader perspective of rent seeking. Therefore, a critical review on the analytical perspective of rent seeking will be given first.

2.1.1 Conventional Theory of Rent-seeking

It is Tullock that first systematically discussed the problem of rent seeking in 1967. In his seminal paper, Tullock (1967) argues that the actual welfare loss of monopoly includes not only the Harberger Triangle but also the Tullock Rectangle because individuals or enterprises who intend to obtain the monopoly rents would use the resources that would otherwise have been used in the productive activities. Tullock did not use the concept of rent seeking and failed to provide a precise definition in that paper. Krueger (1974) created the expression and developed a simple model of competitive rent-seeking in 1974. Buchanan (1980) further distinguishes rent seeking from profit seeking and defines three levels of rent-seeking activity. Tollison (1982) argues that the theory of rent seeking explores how people compete for artificially contrived transfers, and it involves normative and positive elements: the former focuses on the specification and estimation of the costs of rent-seeking activities to the economy while the latter explains the sources of contrived rents in a society. These conventional economists of rent seeking theory, namely Tullock, Buchanan, Tollison and many others, are usually referred to as the Public Choice School. The most comprehensive literature of rent-seeking from Public Choice School comes from Buchanan, James M., Tullock, Gordon & Tollison, Rebort (1980), Lockard & Tullock (2001), Tullock (2005), Congleton, Hillman & Kai (2008), and Congleton & Hillman (2015).

The common use of "rent" refers to a return in excess of a resource owner's opportunity cost. Normally rents emanate from two different sources. They can arise naturally in the price system by shifts in demand and supply curves and such rents are viewed as dissipated quickly because competition will drive them to normal levels. The pursuit of rents of this kind is equivalent to profit seeking (Buchanan, 1980; Tollison,

1982). Rents can also be contrived artificially through government intervention, "Governmental licenses, quotas, permits, authorizations, approvals, franchise assignments: each of these closely related terms implies arbitrary and/or artificial scarcity created by government··· Regardless of the reason, such scarcity implies the potential emergence of rents, which, in turn, implies rent-seeking activity" (Buchanan, 1980:9).

In Buchanan's definition, rent is used in the narrow sense in which only monopoly rents are included, but he intends to emphasize the relationship to government activity in fact. Just as he puts it, "rent-seeking activity is directly related to the scope and range of governmental activity in the economy, to the relative size of the public sector" (Buchanan, 1980:9).[①] Actually, from the outset, Tullock developed rent seeking theory from a broader view including capturing a transfer,[②] to put it differently in Pius Fischer's term (2006:25), i.e. "income without being productive". As Tollison (1982: 577) puts it, "It is this activity of wasting resources in competing for artificially contrived transfers that is called rent-seeking".

① Not all the scholars agree with this argument. Pius Fischer (2007:26) argues that "rent-seeking settings cover a continuum from government-related to strictly private settings where the government plays at the most a very passive role". At one end is protection effectuated by government policy, which is the most evident case of government involvement in rent creation; at the other end, rent seeking takes place in private social life depending on the society's subjective definition of property rights and duties (Pius Fischer, 2007:26~27).

② In Tullock's original paper (1967), he analyzed tariff and monopoly, later focused on transfer (Tullock, 1971; 1974), and then on aid (Tullock, 1975).

Obviously, the Public Choice economists defined rent-seeking in a broader sense, emphasizing the relation between rent-seeking and government activities.① In their definition, rents include not only monopoly rents but also "rent-like transfers (or rents based on transfers)" if we use the term that Khan (Khan & Jomo, 2000:35-40) has suggested in his study on rent seeking.②

On the other hand, they emphasize the waste of resources. They argue that competition for rents generates social waste because resources that could otherwise be devoted to value-producing activities are engaged in competition for distributive results. Based on this, they develop some models to calculate the rent-seeking cost, i.e. the extent of social waste that rent-seeking result in.③ Furthermore a lot of empirical studies to calculate the actual rent-seeking cost in different countries have come out (See Table 1).

---

① As it is stated typically in the first volume of readings on rent-seeking edited by Buchanan, Tollsion and Tullock (1980:Ⅸ), "It (rent seeking) is meant to describe the resource-wasting activities of individuals seeking transfers of wealth *through the aegis of the state.*"

② Khan argues that conventional rent-seeking theory assumes that rent-seeking only results in the creation or protection of monopoly rents. In fact, this is unfair. Public Choice economists include at least the rent-like transfers, as I analyze here.

③ One of most famous is developed by Borsner (1975) in 1975. He argues that the rent-seeking cost equals to the size of the rent itself, i.e. the whole Tullock Rectangle would be wasted. But Tullock (1993) holds a different view arguing that the rent seeking cost either larger than Tullock Rectangle or smaller than it while it is rare to equal to it.

Table 1 Estimates of the Welfare Losses from Rent-seeking

Study	Economy	Year	Welfare loss
Krueger (1974)	India	1964	7% GNP
Krueger (1974)	Turkey	1968	15% GNP(trade sector)
Posner(1975)	United States	various years	3% GNP(regulation)
Cowling and Mueller(1978)	United States	1963.6	13% GCP(private monopoly)
Cowling and Mueller(1978)	United Kingdom	1968.9	7% GCP(private monopoly)
Ross(1984)	Kenya	1980	38% GDP(trade sector)
Mohammad and Whalley(1984)	India	1980.1	25~40% GNP
Laband and Sophocleus(1988)	United States	1985	50% GNP
Lopez and Pagoulatos (1994)	United States	1987	12.5% of domestic consumption

a GCP=gross corporate product.

Source: Adapted from Tollison, 1997:514.

Rent-seeking basically implies a distortion of the market and a waste of productive resources, and the rent-seeking theory seeks to explain the negative consequences for the economic growth of pricing fixing mechanisms by government intervention other than the market (Boyd, 2008). That is, in their analysis, rent-seeking activities are basically negative because they are inefficient and harmful to social welfare, and hence growth-retarding to the economy. Therefore, for the Public Choice economists, to eliminate rent-seeking activities becomes their utmost matter of concern.

About the actors involving in the process of rent-seeking, the Public Choice economists analyze different actors based on methodological individualism. In their model of "competitive rent-seeking" "government" is reduced to "politician" and "bureaucrat", who serves primarily as a broker of the pressures from individuals, enterprises or interest groups of both the demand and the supply sides of the political market.① In the process, those individuals, enterprises or interest groups, as the principal rent seekers, try to influence government for economic gains, while government (politician and bureaucrat), as the rent creators, mediate the competition for rent to maximize their own utilities.

In a word, in their model of "competitive rent seeking", they focus on rent seekers and rent allocators and only confine them to individuals, such as entrepreneurs and politicians, and enterprises or/and interest groups. The traditional conceptions in politics are never seen, such as state, government, power and authority. From this respective, the rent-seeking theory of the conventional Public Choice economists is termed by Boyd as "the liberal market mode of rent utilization" with

① Machesney holds a different view about the role that the politicians play. In the model of "rent extraction", he identifies politicians not as mere brokers but as independent actors getting private actor to respond to their own demands (Machesney, 1987; 1991). In that model, politicians are not rent allocators who redistribute wealth in response to competing private demands, but rent seekers who pursue their own self-defined interest.

a characteristic of political market rent seeking nexus that reflects the particular circumstances of the USA. It may not matter in the United States which is a typical instance of a stateless-society, but problems arise in the other political economy especially in the so-called state-society[①] (Boyd, 2009:255~256).

2.1.2 Rent-seeking in the Developing Countries

Khan & Jomo (2000) find that there are more types of rents and the efficiency and growth effects of different rents are complicated in the developing countries. Khan (Khan & Jomo, 2000:21~69) defines another five types of rents in addition to monopoly rents. They are rent-like transfer (or rent based on transfer), natural resource rent, Schumpeterian rent, rent for learning, and rent for monitoring (or monitoring and management rent). Khan argues that not all the kinds of rents do necessarily result in inefficiency, and some of them may be growth-enhancing (See Table 2). To emphasize the special political and institutional context concerning with rents and rent-seeking, Khan identifies rent-seeking in a much broader sense "as activities which seek to create, maintain or change the rights and institutions on which particular rents are based" connecting rent-seeking to right and institutional change (Khan & Jomo, 2000:5).

① These concepts of state-society and Stateless-society are borrowed from Dyson by Boyd. The former means there is a highly developed sense of public power which is not reducible to the totality of private powers, but the latter does not have such a developed idea and tradition of the state to shape the politics. See Boyd (2009:256).

Table 2 Relevant Growth and Efficiency Implications of Different Rents

Type	Efficiency Implications	Growth Implications	Observations
Monopoly Rent	Inefficient	Likely to be growth-reducing	Sometimes difficult to distinguish from Schumpeterian or leaning rent
Natural Resource rent	Efficient	Likely to be growth-enhancing	
Rent-like Transfer	Neutral, with possible incentive inefficiencies	Indeterminate:may be growth-enhancing	May be essential for primitive accumulation and to maintain political stability,but may also become inefficient very rapidly
Schumpeterian Rent	May be Efficient	Likely to be growth-enhancing	May become monopoly rent if it persists for too long
Rent for Learning	Inefficient	May be growth-enhancing	Efficiency may depend on monitoring and enforcement ability of the state
Rent for Monitoring	May be Efficient	May be growth-enhancing	Efficiency may depend on monitoring and enforcement ability of monitors

Source: Khan & Jomo, 2000:68.

Khan *et al.* also discuss the outcomes of rent seeking. In their model of rent seeking as a process, they examine the net effect of rent-seeking by comparing the "output" (net social benefit associated with the rent-outcome) and the "input" (the rent-seeking cost). They argue that outcomes of rent-seeking are not always inefficient and growth-reducing, and rent-seeking would generate positive outcome under particular political and institutional context.

When he and his fellows do some empirical studies on rent seeking in several Southeastern Asian countries during the period of rapid economic development in the last century, they find that corruption, clientelism and other forms of rent-seeking prevailed in Philippine, Thailand, Malaysia and Indonesia. They point out that many other types of rents except monopoly rents existed in these countries and the implications of seeking for these rents are complicated. Their studies show that the outcomes of rent-seeking heavily depend on the political and institutional variables and the effects of rent-seeking on the economy are much more complicated than what Public Choice economists have exhibited.

By comparing the input and outcome of rent-seeking, he examines the relationship between rent-seeking and economic growth, trying to find out the right political and institutional setting that can create and maintain "good" rents. In essence, Khan's approach shares the same underlying assumption with developmental state theory: economic growth was predicated upon getting the price wrong but the institution right (Ngo, 2009:4). This improves the explanatory ability of rent-seeking theory especially to the reality in developing countries. However, although Khan has drawn a different conclusion from public choice school theory, Khan's approach still suffers from a serious limitation. That is, Khan's approach still exclusively focuses on rent seeking itself.

This situation changes when attention shifted to empirical studies on the rent-seeking in East Asian economies (Yoon, 1991; Cho, 1996; Boyd, 2005, 2006, 2008). Rent creation and allocation are paid attention to in the studies as they were used actively as policy instruments by the governments in the state-led development of those economies. As early as 1991, Korean scholar Yoon (1991:78-97) put forward a broader analytical framework to study the rent-seeking activities in the process of economic growth in Korea. He principally analyzes the mechanism of rent creation and allocation through government intervention based on the premise that government acts as rent creator and rent allocator while private enterprises act as rent seeker.

In the empirical study on rents and rent-seeking in the East Asian countries, Boyd (2006; 2008; 2009) finds out that non-market price-setting and non-market resource allocation prevail in these countries. In those processes, rents and rent-seeking embed in the politics every bit as much as in the economy of the same political economy. When viewed from the political end of the political economy of rent-seeking, the creation of rents, the allocation of rents and rent-seeking itself are part of the normal business of politics. It serves political ends, such as the pursuit of power and the rewarding of supporters, as well as ostensible economic ends. He uses a new term "modes of rent utilization" ① to emphasize the

① Boyd did not suggest the concept of "a mode(s) of rent utilization" from the beginning, and he has developed it for several years in his empirical studies on rent seeking. When he (2002; 2005) first did the comparative studies on rents and economic outcomes of Japan and Taiwan, he found that rent seeking has been widespread in both of them throughout the post-World War Ⅱ period when they have experienced their decades-long fast economic growth. This is obviously contradictory to the model of rent seeking of Public Choice School that focuses on the negative consequences of rent seeking to economic growth. By comparing and contrasting the institutional forms of rent seeking in Japan and Taiwan, Boyd concluded that rent seeking is embedded in politics and serves less to enhance the market and more to satisfy the political and financial interests of the state and its partners. Moreover, he further found that there are systematic differences in the two rent regimes that reflect differences in the processes and practices of the two political economies, and these differences are more significant to economic outcomes than is the amount of the rents involved. When he (2006) did the second case study of comparison of Japan and Mexico, he found again that Mexico has its distinctive features in rent seeking which is very different from that of Japan. So he propored the term of "a mode(s) of rent seeking" , which means the institutionalization of rent seeking with enduring characteristics and persistent patterns. Then in his study (Boyd, 2008; 2009) on rent seeking in China, he started to use "a mode(s) of rent utilization" and "patterns of rent utilization" instead "a mode(s) of rent seeking" . He argued the creation of rents, the allocation of rents and rent seeking itself, are part of the normal business of politics when viewed from the political end of the political economy of rent seeking. And he further extended the hypothesis, arguing that different economy shapes different modes of rent utilization which leads to different political and economic outcomes, and that the mode of rent utilization restricts allocation of rents and effects the costs of rent seeking, even reduces it to nearly zero. Furthermore, he discussed the determinants of modes of rent utilization from formal and informal institutional perspective, namely, the architecture of the state, the social ordering and the government-business relations. Although he admitted modes of rent utilization hinge on a series of factors, such time, space, economic and political ones, he mainly emphasized the political factors partly because they play the most important role and partly because power and politics are missing in the mainstream study on Asian political economy.

institutionalized pattern with enduring characteristics in different political and economic contexts. He argues that the modes of rent utilization differ in different countries, and are significant to economic outcomes. In addition, he discusses the determinants of modes of rent utilization from formal and informal institutional factors. The principal determinants are hypothesized to be the architecture of the state, the mode of social ordering and the government-business relations.

Based on the study of his fellows including Boyd, Ngo (2009; 2010) makes a further advance about this approach by putting forward a similar term "rent production" to emphasize the institutional supply side of rents. By this term, he refers to "the whole range of activities connected to the fabrication of economic rent, including its creation, allocation, extraction, redistribution and pursuit" (Ngo, 2009:10). He conceptualizes the sequence of rent production into three interrelated but separable processes, namely rent creation, rent allocation, and rent-seeking. In each process, the following questions are focused on. "Who are the actors? What kinds of rents and rent-like transfers are involved? What are the ostensible goals? How are rents exchanged?" (Ngo, 2009:11)

Multiple state and market actors including rent creators, allocators, recipients, and seekers are involved in the rent production. In each category, institutional as well as individual actors are included. The government is the main rent creator by virtue of its control over regulatory power and property rights with the power of rent creation and allocation dispersing among competing bureaucratic units. Rent seekers are not only confined to individual actors, typically the private entrepreneurs, but also institutional actors, such as state sectors/ governmental establishments, industrial sectors, business enterprises and so on. It is worth noting that individual government units can be rent-seekers created by central policies or by other bureaucratic establishments while creating their own rents to be allocated to their hand-picked beneficiaries in the case of China (Ngo, 2009:10~12).

Ngo believes that it is possible to trace the sequence of rent production in a specific commodity, industry, policy, or economic sector by locating the sources of rent creation, the means of rent allocation, and the methods of rent-seeking, and so on. In essence, Ngo's model is not dramatically different from Boyd's "modes of rent utilization", because both of them try to broaden the analysis of rent-seeking by integrating the phase of rent creation and rent allocation into the conventional model of rent-seeking.

2.2 Rent-seeking in China's Plan-based Economy

As mentioned in Chapter I, China had been a plan-based economy for a long time that can be divided into two stages: Before Reform with a centrally planned economy and After Reform with a transitional economy under which planning and market co-existed. Most studies on rent-seeking in China focus on the After Reform (1978) Stage (Hu, 1989; He, 1994; Wan, 1999; He & Wang ,1999; Economic System Comparison Editorial Department, 1999; Liu, 2008; Ngo & Wu, 2009; Wu & Ngo, 2010). Only a few studies analyze rent-seeking phenomena Before Reform (Fung,1987; Liu, 2009, 2010; Lin *et al.*, 2003; Wedeman, 2003).

2.2.1 Rent-seeking in the Transitional Economy after Reform

Rent seeking theory was firstly introduced into China by Wu Jinglian and some others in 1988, two years after Buchanan received the Nobel Prize. The initial purpose was to explain the serious corruption phenomena emerged in the process of market-oriented reform (Economic System Comparison Editorial Department, 1999). In addition to introductions or interpretations of this theory, most studies are engaged in estimating the costs of rent-seeking activities in China's transitional economy (Hu, 1989; Wan, 1995; 1998; Hu, 2001), and in the differences of rent seeking between China and the West (He, 1994; He & Wang, 1999; Liu, 2008).

In the hybrid economy After Reform, planning was still a common means for the Chinese government to allocate resources in many aspects of the national economy. Substantial rents were created by government intervention. According to Hu's (1989) estimation, the value of rents created by the dual-track system[①] through control over price, bank loan interest, and foreign exchange rate amounted to RMB[②] 200 billion in 1987, RMB 350 billion in 1988, which accounted for 20% and 30% of the gross national income respectively. Wan (1995) estimates rents created in 1992 after the price reform. The amount of rents arising from the dual-track system had vastly reduced but still amounted to RMB 390 billion, accounting for 19% of the gross national income. Hu (2001:60) points out that rents principally generated from tax loopholes, state investment, revenue erosion, illegal black market and monopoly during the late 1990s, and the welfare loss resulted from rent seeking accounted for 15% of the GDP.[③]

Rent seeking in China at this period is quite different from that in the West. Firstly, the rent-generating sources are different in different institutional settings. Hu (1994) distinguishes three sources of generating rents: government unwitting rent-creating (zhengfu wuyi chuangzu), government passive rent-creating (zhengfu beidong chuangzu) and government active

---

① Under this system, traditional central planning (the plan track) and the emerging product market (the market track) coexisted as means of resource allocation. In particular, an identical good would often be allocated on both the plan track and the market track. The good would typically be sold at a substantially higher price in the market than in the plan.

② RMB (renminbi) is the official name of China currency, literally meaning "people's currency".

③ Hu (2001) estimates the welfare loss resulted by corruption not rent seeking, but there was overlap to a great extent. So this can be seen as the approximation of total rents.

rent-creating (zhengfu zhudong chuangzu).[①] In Western market economy, rents unwillingly created by the government to correct market failure and rents passively created by governments captured by interest groups account for a large proportion while rents actively created by governments are much less than the former two kinds. The political institutions and legal systems mainly determine this difference. In China's transitional economy, most of the rents are actively created by governments, mainly through the two-track systems of prices, policies and the like.

Secondly, the means of rent-seeking is also different in China from the West. In the West, legal means, such as a lobby, is often used by interest groups to affect legislative body to capture monopoly rents. From the perspective of Public Policy, rent-seeking often emerges in the policy decision process. However, illegal means is mostly used in China. Rent seekers often bribe the politician to secure the privilege through "back-door" or give

① Yoon (1991:95-97) in his Ph.D. dissertation suggests a similar model from the perspective of government-business relationship. According to whether governments create rents actively or passively and whether enterprises seek rents actively or passively, there are four different kinds of relations. He and Wang's (1999) analysis is similar to this model, but it seems that he does not mention the first kind in this model.

Government-business Relations Analysis Model

	Government: rent creation		
	Active	Passive	
Enterprise:	Active	Ⅰ	Ⅱ
Rent-seeking	Passive	Ⅲ	Ⅳ

Source: Yoon, 1991:96.

kickback (commission) to them to approach official fixed-price products at a much lower price than the market-clearing level. In China, it is difficult for rent seekers to affect the legislative process and so rent seeking mainly emerges in the process of policy implementation (He, 1994; He &Wang, 1999).

Thirdly, the results of rent-seeking in the economy are also different. The conventional theorists define rent-seeking as a kind of pathology and believe that rent-seeking results in nothing but social loss and therefore retards economic growth. Liu (2008:237~239) argues that rent-seeking has two different kinds of effects on the transitional economy in China. On the one hand, rent-seeking leads to social loss as the conventional theorists point out; on the other hand, rent-seeking deepens the reform and promotes economic growth. The incremental reform led by the Chinese government is a process of trial and error accompanied by rent-seeking. During the reform without a blueprint characterized by experimentation, the demand for institutional reform always comes first, and then the related institution is designed to experiment and virtually implemented while being revised from times to times. In this process of "groping for stepping stones to cross the river", institution supply always lags behind institution demand, therefore the prevalence of rent-seeking is inevitable.

Recently scholars from Leiden-Tsinghua project have furthered the study on rent-seeking in post-reform China.① They discuss rents and rent seeking in the process of China's industrial development focusing on rent creation, rent allocation and rent seeking from a broader approach. They find two distinct features in transitional China's industrial development. One is that rent-seeking activities principally occur between state-owned enterprises (SOEs) and governments. Substantial rents that created by governments, intentionally or unintentionally, principally flow into the relevant SOEs. The other is that local governments act as rent seekers as well as rent creators. In order to promote local development, local governments and the bureaucrats seek all kinds of rents on the national level from the central government to their jurisdictions on one hand, and they create various kinds of rents for enterprises in their own jurisdictions on the other hand (Boyd, 2008; Ngo & Wu, 2009; Wu & Ngo, 2010). However, they fail to extend their studies to the Before Reform Stage of the centrally planned economy.

2.2.2 Rent-seeking in the Centrally Planned Economy before Reform

Many studies deny the existence of rent-seeking activities, even the existence of rents, in the centrally planned economy before Reform. They argue that, under the centrally planned economic system, almost all the

① Dominated by Ngo, Tak-Wing and Wu, Yongping, tens of scholars in this Leiden-Tsinghua project have devoted themselves to rent seeking in post-reform China. As the concrete results of their joint project, two volumes were printed in 2009 and 2010 respectively. See Ngo & Wu (2009) and Wu & Ngo (2010).

production factors were controlled by the central government and their production and distribution were strictly implemented according to the plan. Under such circumstance, individual ministry and local governments did not have their own interests and there was no need to seek rents (Hu,1994; Liu, 2008: 164~173).

The reason for their argument is that it is neither market failure nor government failure but the coordination failure between market and government function that leads towards the rent-seeking society. In their opinion, there are no rent-seeking activities both in the perfect free market with "a small government" and in the centrally planned economy with an "almighty government". The boundary between market and government changes dynamically over time and the coordination failure between them under a mixed economy of modern society is the basic reason for rent-seeking activity (He, 1994; He & Wang, 1999).

On the contrary, some studies show that a special type of rent had already emerged in the centrally planned economy Before Reform (Fung, 1987; Hu, 2009, 2010; Lin et al., 2003; Wedeman, 2003:60~68). In a market economy where à la Tullokian rent-seeking model originated, rent arises from a price gap between the market-clearing price and the higher price artificially fixed by the state. However, in the centrally planned economy of China, rent arises in essence from a price gap between the market-clearing price and the lowered price artificially depressed by the state (See Figure 1).① Fung (1987) firstly conceptualized it as "surplus", and accordingly identified the activity capturing such kind of rent as "surplus seeking" in contrast to rent-seeking.② "Surplus" comes from the direct price control. In theory, the beneficiaries are the buyers who receive the rationed goods at a lowered price (Fung, 1987; Hu, 2009), but the state is the monopolistic legitimate owner of the rents (Wedeman, 2003:60~68). However, which individual or industry can get the rationed goods and at what price depend on the political authority and responding institutional arrangement in the planned economic context. In this sense, this type of rent can be termed as "institutional rent" (Lin *et al.*, 2004:210~214).

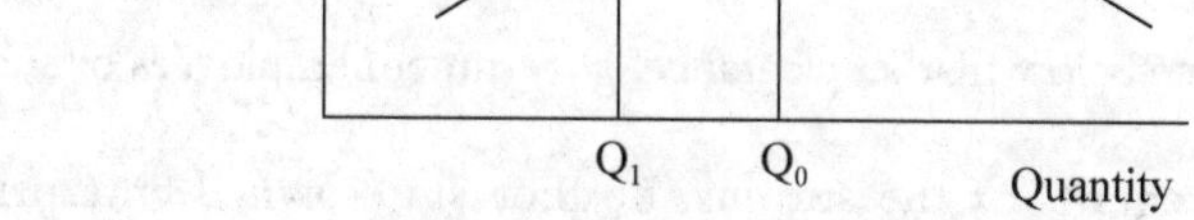

Figure 1 Institutional Rent under a Low-Price Control

---

① This aspect is commonly recognized also by Fung (1987), Hu (2009, 2010), Lin et al. (1994, 2003), although termed slightly differently.

② Although Hu (2009, 2010) uses the same terms with Fung (1987), there is a difference. In Hu's definition, surplus refers to price gap between the original price and the depressed price showed as showed in Figure 1.

Albeit a consensus that substantial institutional rents exited in China's centrally planned economy, a divergence of argument on rent seeking is among different scholars.

Lin et al. (2003:210~214) argue that rent seeking by individuals and enterprises was uncommon due to a low motivation under tight institutional constraints, but rent-seeking activities did exist. As for rent seeking by individuals, in their opinion, "what did exist at the time were only the activities to acquire resources through personal relations" (Lin *et al.*, 2003:212), while "rent-seeking of enterprises were only intended to expand their business" (Lin *et al.*, 2003:211).

Fung (1987) holds a different view, arguing that "surplus seeking" through "back-door deals" by the dominant method of exchange of favors was wide-spread in the planned economy. Hu (2009) further believed that institutional players besides the individuals and enterprises could be the rent seekers, as he states , "After the government creates the surplus through fixing a price below market clearance, government employees or subordinates seek the benefits of the surplus, be they state-owned enterprises, local governments, or bureaus."

In short, although all these studies on rent seeking in the centrally planned economy support the emergence of "rents" , they do not hold the same view on whether there were substantial "rent-seeking" activities at that time. Moreover, all these analyses tend to become theoretical rather than empirical, failing to provide empirical studies based on historical fact.

2.3 Analytical Model of Rent Utilization for the Plan-based Economy

2.3.1 Institutional Context for the Analytical Model

This study is to analyze what roles the governments, central and local, and enterprises of all types play in China's auto industrial development in the plan-based economy from a broader perspective of rent-seeking. The traditional wisdom only focuses on the single term of rent-seeking. In the rent-seeking model, "government" is identified as rent creator and individuals, enterprises or interest group as rent seekers. However, rent-seeking in China tells a different story. To set up an analytical framework for this study, China's practical and institutional context should be considered.

Firstly, in China's political and economic context, not only is rent-seeking activity closely connected to the governmental activity, but also rent per se is considered as a policy instrument. In the reality of China's economic development, the state itself has always been the dominant force. In order to fulfill its development strategy or industrial policy, the state intentionally creates rents through the political system and distributes them by corresponding institutional arrangements to the target groups. In both of these rent creation and rent allocation processes, rent seeking is inevitable. Thus the creation, allocation, and seeking of rents have been embedded in the regulatory framework which governs the economic and industrial development through intimately connecting to the political system (Ngo, 2008). From this sense, we can term all the activities revolving around rents, that is, rent creation, rent allocation and rent seeking, as "rent utilization".

Secondly, multiple state and market actors are involved in the process of rent utilization. As the main creator and legitimate owner of rents, the state disperses the authority of rent-creation and allocation in governments of different levels, and both central and local governments play critical roles in rent utilization in China's political and economic context. In particular, the central government acts as rent creator and allocator, and the local governments act as rent creator and allocator as well as rent seeker at the same time. At the national level, local governments act as rent allocator and rent seeker, and at the local level, local governments act as rent creator and allocator. In both situations, enterprises of all kinds are rent seekers.

2.3.2 Analytical Model of Rent Utilization

In China's political and economic context, rent utilization, the term describing all the activities revolving around rents, can be divided into three different but sometimes overlapped aspects: rent creation, rent allocation, and rent-seeking.

In particular, the analytical model of rent utilization in this study is described in Figure 2.

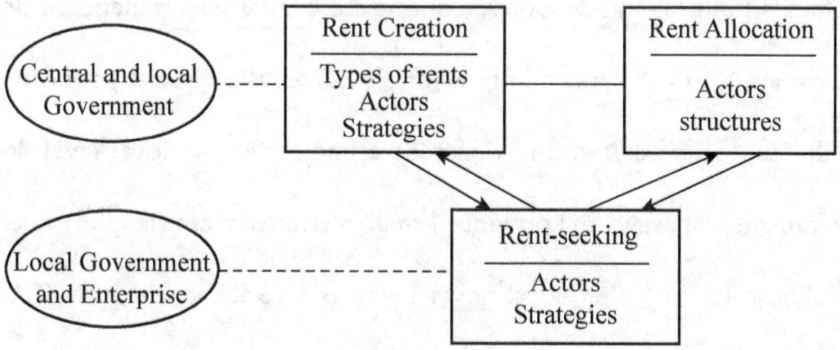

Figure 2 Analytical Model of Rent Utilization

The actors of rent creation in China's political economy context include the central government and local governments of different levels. In the case of auto industry, different kinds of rents are created intentionally or unintentionally at the central level by industrial policy and relative intervention. At the local level, the local governments often make their own development plans and intervene in the auto industrial development by different means creating different kinds of rents for enterprises in their own jurisdictions to obtain their self-defined interests.

Generally, it is common to use price control, entry restriction, quantity restriction and financial supporting as the means of rent creation. Monopoly rent is often created through entry restriction, and surplus generally comes from price control, but there is no one-to-one correspondence between types of rent and the means. It is common that the combination of these means is used at the same time.

As for the rent allocation, this study mainly discusses who allocates rents to whom by what structure. As mentioned above, the actors of rent allocation in China's political and economic context are central government and local governments. As the most important allocator, the central government has the authority scattered in different agencies. At the local level, local governments, especially the province-level governments are also the principal rent allocators. In China, local government is a concept with complicated meanings. Generally, it refers to the executive branches of Province (region), City (prefecture-level), County and Township. However, considering China's party-state system, the local Committees of Chinese Communist Party (CCP) paralleling in the four levels of local governments, and they play a critical role in the locals in fact, so local governments are used hereafter in the broad sense. In the case of auto industry, provincial governments are involved most and prefecture-level and county-level governments are also involved much, but most of the time, local governments are considered as a whole in this study.

In the auto industry, the structure of rent allocation is highlighted because it has great effects on rent-seeking. The different structure in different stages in the auto industry is described.

As for rent-seeking, This study discusses who seek rents by what means or strategies. Rent-seeking is viewed in a broad way as activities that individual or institutional actors invest resources (time, energy, money, etc.) to directly secure these kinds of rents and rent-like transfers or to attempt to create or change the rights and institutions on which these rents and transfer-based rents are based. On the one hand, rents are exogenous because rent seekers secure the rents that have been created through the political system in the policy-making process. In this situation, governments actively create and allocate rents as an incentive to induce related actors to fulfill its economic goal in different development stages. On the other hand, rents are endogenous as well because in some situations the rent seekers try to create or change rights or institutional arrangements on which rents are based to indirectly secure the rents. Rent-seeking activities emerge in both stages of policy implementation and the policy-making stage.

Different stages have different types of rent seekers. As the dominating power that promotes local economic and industrial development, local governments seek rents and transfer-based rents at the national level from the central government in order to obtain more fiscal revenue and political promotion. Several common means used by local governments are discussed. As another type of rent seekers, enterprises of all kinds employ several kinds of means as well.

Ⅲ. Rent Utilization in China's Auto Industry: Before Reform

3.1 The Development of Auto Industry in the Centrally Planned Economy before Reform

Under the traditional planned economy system in Before Reform stage, Chinese central government itself directly created its auto industry by establishing State-Owned Enterprises (SOEs) following the way of the Soviet Union. Although the auto industry benefited a lot from the rent-producing macro-policy in obtaining investments and materials under supply shortage, the auto industry developed in a zigzag with a low level of production capability and technology under planned economy system.

Considering the importance of the auto industry to the national economy and military mobility, the newly born China government moved quickly to create its own auto industry.① China planned to build large-scale stated owned auto enterprises under the direct control of the central government, following the way of Soviet Union. China started to build The First Auto Works (FAW) with the help of Soviet Union in 1953, and the first truck was produced in 1956 under the brand of "liberation (Jiefang)". In 1958, a limousine model named "red flag (Hongqi)" was made and since then "Hongqi" has become the famous homegrown brand to service the top-ranking leaders.②

During the "Great Leap Forward" movement (1958 to 1960), some local state-owned auto factories were built thanks to the first-time reform of decentralization. Four of them were built in Beijing, Shanghai, Nanjing, and Jinan which have become the main auto manufacturing bases since then. It is worth noting that a sedan named "phoenix (Fenghuang)" was made for middle-level cadres by Shanghai Auto Factory and then was renamed "Shanghai".

From the mid-1960s, with the increasing military demand for motor vehicles,③ the Chinese government started to build new truck factories in

① On the auto industry before 1949 in China, see Harwit (1995:15-16).

② FAW made a sedan at first named "Dongfeng (East wind) CA71" in 1958, and soon after improved it into a luxury limousine, renaming it "Hongqi CA72".

③ As relations with the Soviet Union deteriorated in the early 1960s, the Chinese leaders worried about the susceptibility of FAW to foreign attack. On the other hand, China was involved in some other wars such as the border war between China and India in 1962 and the Vietnam War in 1965.

relatively isolated mountainous inland regions. Sichuan Auto Works and Shaanxi Auto Works were built to manufacture military off-road vehicles. The building of Second Auto Works (SAW) was also approved, which was ultimately finished in 1978.

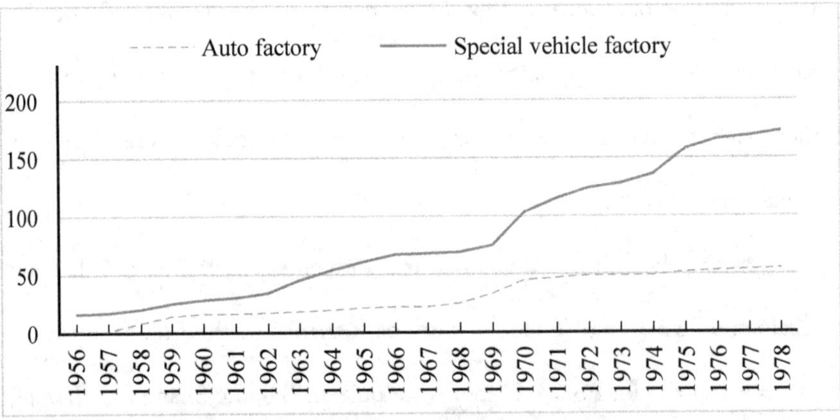

Figure 3 Number of Auto Plants and Special Vehicle Factories 1956~1978
Source: China automotive industry yearbook, 1992:94.

From 1969, the second wave of building local state-owned enterprises started. All of the provinces except Tibet and Qinghai established their own auto factories and auto parts factories, but most of the parts could only be used for the vehicles made in the same locality (Yang, 2003; Liu, 2003). By the end of 1978, the number of auto factories increased to 55, producing various types of trucks and buses, and there were 173 special vehicle factories, making different kinds of special utility vehicles (See Figure 4). The auto production amounted to 149,062, of which sedans accounted for 2,640, merely about 1.77% (See Figure 5).

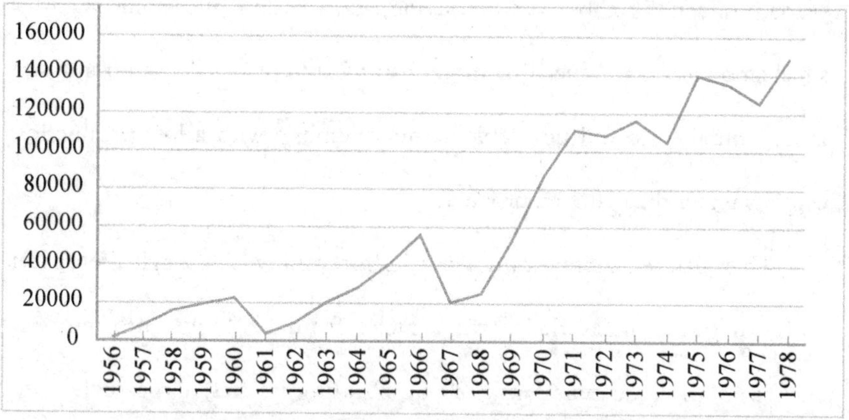

Figure 4 Output of Automobiles, 1956~1978

Source: China automotive industry yearbook, 2009:46.

Before the market-oriented reform, there were several characteristics of the auto industry. Firstly, the staple products were trucks, some buses and only a few sedans with homegrown brands. A small number of "red flag (Hongqi)" sedans were produced by FAW for top leaders, a few "Shanghai" sedans for middle-level cadres. Secondly, like many other manufacturing sectors, the auto industry had a highly scattered and fragmented structure. During that time almost every province, further down to each prefecture and even to each county, had a relatively complete auto industry facility. Thirdly, most of the auto factories were small in scale, with a low production capability and backward technology.

In fact, the actual development of the auto industry was quite different from the initial goal. It took about 25 years from 1953 to 1978 to increase the yearly production to about 150 thousand, and what's more astonishing, this small amount was produced by more than 55 auto plants. The auto industry in the initial stage did not achieve much, ending with a low production capacity under the scattered production.

This differed dramatically from its forerunner. Although the Soviet Union began to make their own vehicles from 1924, the auto industry started in the true sense in 1929 by building its first large-scale auto manufacturing plant, which was also governed in the form of SOE under the direct control of the central government. Only 10 years later in 1939, the auto production already amounted to 200 thousand units, and there were no more than 5 main auto factories (not including special vehicle factories). About 28 years later in 1957, the production hit 495 thousand and only about 5 new auto plants (not including special vehicle factories) increased.[①]

3.2 Rents and Rent Creation

In this initial stage when China was under capital-scarce situation since its very foundation, China government adopted a heavy-industry-oriented development strategy in 1953 which is termed by Lin et al. (2003:29~67)

① About the details of the auto industry in Soviet Union, see Ji (1985).

as "the leap-forward strategy." ① In order to lower the costs for development of heavy industries characterized with a capital-intensity, the central government had to suppress artificially the capital formation costs. Therefore, macro-policy tools with distorted prices were implemented by artificially lowering the prices of credit, foreign exchange, energy, raw materials, labor and so on.

Thus, a great many rents, a special form of "surplus", were created. A "surplus" refers to the price gap between the market-clearing price and the artificially lowered price fixed by the government (Ngo, 2008, 2009, 2010). Different from monopoly rent, surplus rents come from direct price control. In theory, the beneficiaries are the buyers who receive the rationed goods at a lowered price (Fung, 1987; Hu, 2009), but the state is the monopolistic legitimate owner of the rents (Wedeman, 2003:60~68). However, which individual or industry can get the rationed goods at what price depends

① In their opinion, the trinity of the traditional economic system per se, namely the distorted macro policy environment, the planned resource allocation mechanism, and the puppet-like micro-management institutional system including the SOEs and People's Communes, originated endogenously from the so-called "the leap-forward strategy". This is true to a large extent in the case of China. China maintained a market-based economy until roughly 1953 under the guidance of New Democracy in the very beginning, and did not finished establishing the centrally planned economic system by the late 1950s after China decided to adopt a the heavy-industry-oriented development strategy in 1953. See Hu (2008:108~121). Although this analysis overlooked the political factors, especially the decisive role of the Communist Party of China (CPC) whose ideological commitment forced it to follow the powerful forerunner, the Soviet Union in the formation of traditional economic system, it is a logically consistent explanation as a whole.

on the political authority and responding institutional arrangement in the planned economic context. In this sense, surplus rent can be termed as "institutional rent" (Lin *et al.*, 2004:210~214).

Regarded as one section of the general heavy industries, the auto industry under this political economy context was running under the same situation. Institutional rents, particularly in the auto industry, were created mainly in forms of (i) interest rates of bank loans, (ii) foreign exchange rates, and (iii) price gap of products.

The first kind of institutional rents, the interest rates in bank loans, was caused by a low interest-rate policy.[①] In order to develop the capital-intensive heavy industries including auto industry requiring long construction cycle, a low interest rate was maintained for the whole plan-economy stages (See Table 3). In May 1950, the monthly rate of industrial credit fell down to a normal level of 3.0%. However, in the following years, the interest rates were adjusted quite a few times and fell dramatically (Zheng, 1991:115~120).

The second kind of institutional rents, the foreign exchange rates between the official and the market, was created by a low-exchange-rate policy (See Table 4). In the initial stage of development in China, foreign exchange was as scarce as capital because exportable goods were highly

① This kind of rent was also frequently used in other countries, such as South Korea. See Kang(2002), Lee & Cheong(2010).

limited. However, a lot of capital-intensive equipment for heavy industries needed to be imported, requiring payments in foreign exchanges. Therefore, if the foreign exchange rate had been determined by the market, it would have cost the auto industries too much. To ensure that the key projects could import critical equipment at low prices, the central government continued to suppress foreign exchange rate by artificially overvaluing domestic currency ever since 1950. In a little more than one year from March 1950 to May 1951, the exchange rate of RMB against U.S. dollar was adjusted downward 15 times (Lin *et al.*, 2003:42).

Table 3 Interest Rate of Industrial Credit Adjustments (Monthly rate)

Date	Monthly rate (%)	Extent of Adjustment (%)
May, 1950	3.0	—
July 31, 1950	2.0	–1.0
April, 1951	1.5~1.6	–0.5~–0.4
January, 1953	0.6~0.9	–0.9~–0.7
January, 1954	0.456	–0.14~–0.444
June, 1960	0.6	0.144
August, 1971	0.42	–0.16

Source: Zheng, 1991:115~120.

Table 4 Exchange Rate Adjustments(US$100 and Sterling £100=RMB ¥)

Date	U.S.Dollars		Pounds Sterling	
	Exchange rate	Extent of adjustment (%)	Exchange rate	Extent of adjustment (%)
March 13,1950	420.00	—	—	—
July 1,1950	375.0	–10.71	989.00	—
July 8,1950	360.00	–4.00	956.00	–3.34
July 26,1950	360.00	0.00	932.00	–2.51
August 7,1950	350.00	–2.78	914.40	–1.89
September 5,1950	322.00	–8.00	812.20	–11.18
May 23,1951	223.00	–30.75	—	—
December 1971	246.18	10.39	—	—
July 1978	172.00	–39.07	—	—

Source: Lin *et al*, 2003:42.

The third kind of institutional rents, the price gap, was created by price control in varieties of products. During the traditional economic system, the price most products, especially the agricultural products, energy and raw materials, were under the control of the government. In 1953, the State Planning Commission (SPC) was established to fulfill the heavy industry strategy by implementing the low-price-control policy. The commission classified the materials into three categories: (1) Category Ⅰ, materials under unified allocation of the state and ministries; (2) Category Ⅱ, materials under allocation by state industrial ministries and commissions under the State Council; and (3) Category Ⅲ, materials under the allocation of the local administration. From 1953 to 1957, Category Ⅰ materials increased from

110 to 231 items, while Category Ⅱ materials increased from 227 to 301 (Wang, 2010). The main energy materials such as coal, hard coke, steel and iron used in the auto industries belonged to Category Ⅰ whose price were fixed artificially at a lower level.

As one important section of the general heavy industries, the auto industry was running under the same situation in this political and economic context. These three kinds of rents were also applied in the auto industry that attracted great attention from the top-level leaders and benefited from the rent-producing macro-policy by comparatively easily obtaining the investment, foreign exchanges, and raw materials that were generally in short supply. For the auto industry, the investment by the government, central and local, was RMB 0.546 billion from 1953 to 1957, accounting for 0.86% of the national total investment, and the investment increased to RMB 2.257 billion, accounting for 0.99% of the national total investment in the late years of this stage (China Automotive Industry Yearbook, 2009: 45). Thus, the related auto enterprises benefited a lot in the capital-scarce context. In the initial stage to build its own auto industry, China imported large-sized machines and equipment that could not be manufactured by Chinese factories. 80% of the processing equipment for manufacturing trucks was imported from the Soviet Union when FAW was built in the late 1950s, and Sichuan Auto Works also imported manufacturing technologies and processing equipment for heavy-duty trucks from Berliet in France in 1965 (Sun, 2009). These enterprises received a large sum of rents in the form of foreign exchange rates. The target auto enterprises also benefited from the raw materials with large price gap. For example, steel is one of the most import raw materials for auto industry, and it was reported that the target auto enterprises could get steel at 50%~70% of the market price in the late 1950s and the early 1960s (Fu, 1993).

3.3 Rent Allocation

Rent in the first stage was mainly in form of surplus bound to all kinds of resources. In the centrally planned economy, "the 'state' extracts rents from producers and consumers by controlling purchasing, production, and distribution. Rents, however, are only monetized when a finished product is sold to a consumer. Prior to that, rents derived from both the underpricing of inputs and overpricing of outputs exist only in theoretical terms" (Wedeman, 2003:64-65). Therefore, the ultimate realization of rents cannot depend only on the state per se but calls for the division of labor and cooperation among the three separate agents of procurement and manufacturing and distribution. The procurement and manufacturing agents actually pass along a "shadow rent" to the distribution agent who then monetizes the rent and then deposits the cash rent in the state's coffers controlled by the central government, and each of them may ultimately obtain a share of the rents they generate and monetize. This process needs tight control by the central government because each of them can obtain a greater share by hijacking the rents rather than passing them intact. Even with a little bit of relaxation of control, each of these agents could become a rent seeker.

In order to fulfill the heavy-industry-oriented development strategy by utilizing these rents, China adopted a centrally planned economic system to realize the tight control, following the way of Soviet Union. Under the orthodox centrally planned economic system such as the Soviet Union, the centrally planned mechanism was based on a U-form in which hierarchical information flow and control were organized into a unitary form by functional or specialization principle, and the authority was in the hand of a unitary agency of central government. In such a system, "most enterprises were grouped by industry and under the direct supervision of ministries, and regional governments were primarily subordinates of the center and their roles were limited to collecting information from below and implementing plans from above without much autonomy" (Qian & Xu, 1993).

For the auto industry, the Soviet Union set up a particular unitary ministry under the central government to govern the whole auto industry in the late 1920s. Although the name of this agency changed over time,① it had an extensive and centralized authority of governing the whole auto sector. It took charge of all the authority of procuring, manufacturing and distributing for the whole auto industry, and built state-owned auto factories by types of automobiles with a tight

① In the late 1940s, it was called the Ministry of Auto Industry, or Ministry of Auto Industry and Agricultural Machine for some time.

control over the number of total auto enterprises (Ji, 1985; Jia, 2003). In other words, the authority of rent allocation was in only one single agency. By so doing, it intended to diminish the fierce political contention over the authority of rent allocation and make good use of specialization and economies of scale, therefore promote a fast development of the auto industry.

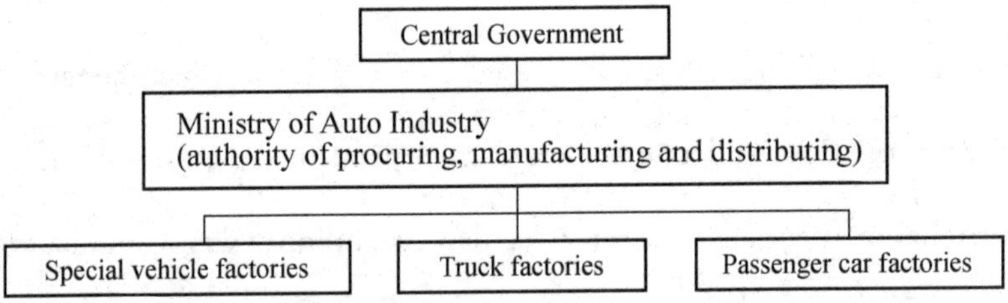

Figure 5 Governing Structure of Soviet Union's Auto Industry

3.3.1 Fragmented Structure of Rent Allocation in the Central Level

Like the Union, China also adopted a similar institutional arrangement to allocate rents. China established the vertical lines of authority based on function over various sectors reaching down from the ministries of the central government. The First Ministry of Machine-Building (FMMB) built in 1952 took charge of the auto industrial development.[①] However, as the competent authority of governing the

① One year after the foundation of PRC in 1949, China built a preparatory office for auto industry under the Ministry of Heavy Industry. In 1952, the First Ministry of Machine Building (FMMB) was established to take charge of developing civilian machinery production. The preparatory Bureau for auto industry was changed into Auto Industry Administrative Bureau (AIAB) under FMMB in charge of the whole development of auto industry.

auto industry, FMMB did not have a centralized governing authority like its counterpart in the Soviet Union. During most time of this period, FMMB only had a partial authority of governing manufacturing agents, while the authority of procuring and distributing was scattered in different agencies under the central government.

As one of the most important heavy industrial sectors, the auto industry was built from a completely new central SOE (that is FAW) under the direct charge of the FMMB.① However, FMMB did not control all the auto-related enterprises from the beginning. When the preparatory office for the auto industry was first set up, only 6 auto-parts factories which had been subordinated to the Chinese People's Liberation Army, Ministry of Heavy Industry and Ministry of Transport (MOT) were transferred to it. This was less than 1/5 of the total 31 auto related enterprises including 9 special vehicle plants and 22 auto-parts factories (China Automotive Industry Yearbook, 1992: 94). In other words, as the governing industrial ministry for the auto industry, FMMB only directly controlled FAW and several other auto-parts factories.

FMMB did not take charge of the authority of procuring for the auto

① Based mainly on a vertical integration principle, the newly built FAW (finished by 1956) subordinated almost all the auto parts factories to its assembly factory with an exception of an auto-parts factory built in Beijing far away from Changchun, the site of its assembly factory. In other words, the FAW internalized most of the auto-parts factories. The exception, Beijing FAW parts factory, was set as an independent enterprise, and it was also in the direct charge of the FMMB as a central SOE.

industry. The procurement agent then was Materials Bureau under the direct control of the central government, for the input for auto industry including energy (such as electricity, coal, and hard coke) and raw materials (such as steel, pig iron) belonged to Category I under unified allocation of the state. The Materials Bureau was the supremely important agent because it was identified as an agent for providing materials base for the whole centrally planned economy. At first it was set under the State Planning Commission (SPC) in 1953, the critical planning agent that was a super ministry headed by a vice premier, and then it was transferred in the following years between the SPC and the State Economic Commission (SEC), which was another super ministry responsible for the implementation and supervision of the decided planning. As one of the most important agents that realized the rents for the central government, the Materials Bureau was always under the tight control of the central government although its controlling authority was changed from time to time.① This indicates that the procurement agent per

① In fact, as Materials Bureau controlled the most important authority of distributing energy and raw-materials and the rents with them, fierce political contention revolved around the controlling authority of it in the whole process of the planned economy, which could be showed in the continuous transfers of the materials bureau between the SPC and the SEC in the first years. Materials Bureau was firstly put under the SPC in 1953, and it was transferred to SEC in May 1956, and then transferred back to SPC in September 1958. In August 1959, it was again transferred to SEC. In May 1963, it was upgraded to a State Materials General Bureau in the direct charge of the State Council, and in September 1964, it was further upgraded to a ministry. In June 1970, it was degraded and put under SPC again. In November 1975, it was set as a state general bureau with a higher administrative rand (Fu, 1993).

se had a strong motivation to abandon its role as the agent of the state's rent realization system and became egoistic rent seeker.①

The distribution agent was the last and most important agent to realize the rents. The possibility of rent-seeking by the distribution agent was relatively high because the shadow rent in the form of auto parts and finished automobiles doubled and it could hijack the monetized double rents by simply embezzling them. What is more, automobiles were identified as a means of production due to a serious shortage for a long time and put under the Category Ⅰ of materials under unified allocation of the state. Thus, the competition for the authority of distributing auto products was very furious.

Most of the time, Materials Bureau took charge of the authority to distribute completed autos while Ministry of Transport (MOT) was responsible for the production and sales of auto parts. Before China could manufacture its own automobiles, it was the Ministry of Commerce

① In theory, the Materials Bureau could divert the undervalued energy and raw materials to the "black market" and sell them at a higher price to monetize the shadow rents, but in the early years, the possibility of rent-seeking by the Materials Bureau in the central level was relatively low in reality. For one thing, it was of strategic priority to build the large-scale auto industry and the Materials Bureau should follow this preference; for another, the Materials Bureau was under strict supervision of the central government. Of course, the possibility of rent seeking of the individuals who hold the authority of distributing energy and raw-materials was relatively high, but as was analyzed by Lin *et al.* (2003:210~212), this kind of rent-seeking activities was uncommon due to institutional constraints under the traditional economic system.

(MOC), the state commercial agency then, that took charge of distributing the imported automobiles, but in 1957 after FAW began to produce trucks, the authority of distributing finished automobiles was transferred to MOT. The direct reason was that most of the auto products, only in the form of trucks, were used in the transportation area, but what was behind was the substantial rents along with finished automobiles. In 1961, the authority of distributing the finished automobiles was put under the Materials Bureau, which sold them through its province-level agents.① From then, the Materials Bureau became the procurement agent and the distribution agent at the same time for the auto industry. However, MOT captured the sale of auto-parts from MOC and the authority of planning and producing the auto parts from FMMB.② In 1964, China did try to concentrate the governing authority. China National Automotive Industry Corporation (CNAIC) was set up in place of AIAB under FMMB to govern the whole auto industry, including the planning and producing of finished automobiles and auto parts. Nevertheless, it still did not have the intact authority. Although it obtained the authority of

① Under Materials Bureau was established Mechanical and Electrical Equipment Company (MEEC) for the sale of finished vehicles and other mechanical and electrical products, and 28 branches were set up in the provincial level under its vertical management (Liu, 2003).

② MOT established two different agencies for governing auto-parts production and sales of auto-parts. It took over all the agencies under MOC for sale of auto-parts and built 6 branches in Tianjin, Shenyang, Shanghai, Guangzhou, Chongqing and Xi'an (Liu, 2003).

sale of auto-parts and took over all the distribution function of MOT, sales of finished automobiles was still in the hand of the Materials Bureau. Unfortunately, even this relatively centralized structure did not last for long because of the Cultural Revolution, a communism-re-strengthening political movement from 1966, brought serious chaos in all the areas of the society.① After 1969, the authority of sales of auto parts was again scattered in three different agencies: MOT, Materials Bureau and FMMB.

In a word, the rent allocation structure at the central level for the auto industry was very fragmented from the beginning. Compared with the Soviet Union, FMMB under such a fragmented structure could not enforce a strict control over the auto industry. Through multiple authorities, it was much easier for rent-seeking activities to occur.

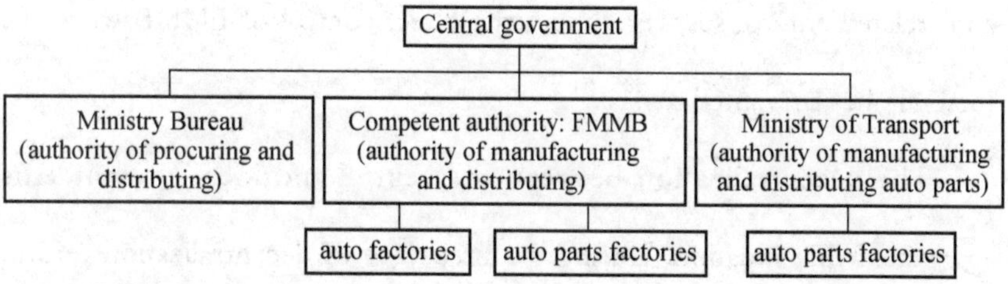

Figure 6　Fragmented Structure of Rent Allocation in the Central Level

① In fact, CNAIC was like a kind of trust of finished auto plants and auto-parts factories. It had 4 auto branch companies in Changchun, Beijing, Nanjing and Chongqing, with 1 auto-bearing branch company, 2 general auto plants in Ji'nan and Wuhan, and the Auto-parts Company which was responsible for the sale of auto-parts. About the details of CNAIC, See Chen (2003) and Liu (2003).

3.3.2 Multilayered Structure of Rent Allocation between Central Level and Local Level

The authority of planning and governing auto industry was also shared between the central government and local governments from the very beginning. As the governing industrial ministry for the auto industry, FMMB governed directly only FAW and several other auto-parts factories at the beginning. In addition, some special purpose vehicle factories and auto-parts factories already existing in Shanghai and other cities were not under the charge of FMMB. By 1957, the local special purpose vehicle plants had increased to 17, and the auto-parts factories (including motorcycle-components enterprises) had increased to 95 (*China automotive industry yearbook,* 1992:94). Only a few of these enterprises were under the direct control of the FMMB. Even in the most centralized time in 1964, only 75 auto related enterprises were under the direct control of FMMB while the total number amounted to 417.①

The decentralization between the central and local governments aggravated this situation. During the first wave of decentralization reform from 1958 to 1960, most of the central auto related enterprises except for FAW and Nanjing Auto plants were transferred to the local governments. During the second wave of administrative decentralization from the late

① The former number comes from Chen (2003), while the latter number comes from China Automotive Industry Yearbook, 1994:65.

1960s, most of the auto plants and parts factories including FAW were in the charge of local governments. The authority of planning, procuring, governing producing and distributing also was divided between the central and the provincial governments. The production of automobiles under the planning of the FMMB used materials from the central materials agency, and correspondingly the automobiles were distributed by the central materials agency. On the contrary, the production under local governments' planning used the materials from local governments and the distributing authority was also in the hand of local governments (Liu, 2003).

In other words, there was a multilayered structure of rent allocation in the auto industry between the central government and local governments. This complicated structure made it much difficult to control over local governments of different levels due to the inherent information asymmetry and geographical remoteness.

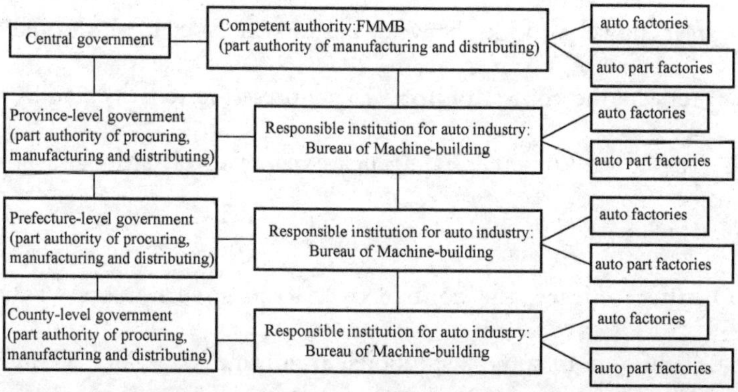

Figure 7 Multilayered Structure of Rent Allocation between Central and Local Level

3.3.3 Institutional Arrangements of Local Governments Being Rent–seekers

Rent in the first stage was mainly in form of surplus bound to all kinds of resources. The state, as the rent creator, extracts this kind of rent through a whole set of mechanism. In essence, the state per se was an elaborate, though not perfect, device of creating and allocating rents, and the local governments and the other related agencies were just "cogs" of this device. This process of rent realization needs tight control by the central government because each of "cogs" could play as latent rent seeker even with a little bit of relaxation of control. It depends on the control mechanism whether or not one agent could become a rent seeker (Wedeman, 2003:64~65). The agents of procurement and distribution, which are the two ends in the continuum process of rent realization, showed dramatic changes.① On the one hand, this indicates that the contention of rent seeking by these two agents was so fierce that a great "power struggle" between the two ends occurred. On the other hard, it reflects the constant efforts to suppress the rent seeking by these agents. The control over central agencies was relatively strict and possible despite a high cost.

On the contrary, the control over local governments was much more difficult due to some institutional arrangements besides the inherent information asymmetry and geographical remoteness. The first institutional

① About the details of these two agents in the auto industry, see pp.34~35.

arrangement is the relationship between central and local governments. Although a centrally planned economic system was adopted by the state in that stage, the existence of an "M-form hierarchical structure" (Qian & Xu, 1993) made local governments own some autonomies which in turn eracted them to seek rents. With such a structure different from a U-form[①] by functional or specialization principle in the Soviet Union, "the Chinese economy is organized into a 'multi-layered-multi-regional form' mainly according to territorial principle, in which each region at each layer can act as a separate operating unit. Each unit is further divided along geographic lines and at the same time controls its own enterprises along functional and specialization principle. Regions are relatively self-contained; that is, they are self-sufficient in terms of functions and supplies in production" (Qian & Xu, 1993). In China of that time, there were six administrative levels: central, provincial, prefecture, county, commune (subsequently, township) and brigade (subsequently, village). Moreover, there were three levels in urban areas: municipality, district and neighborhood. Although each functional or industrial bureau in a region is subject to "dual leadership" of the regional

① The "U-form" means a unitary form organized by functional or specialization principle in Soviet Union. Under this form, the authority was in the hand of a unitary agency of central government. In such a system, "most enterprises were grouped by industry and under the direct supervision of ministries, and regional governments were primarily subordinates of the center and their roles were limited to collecting information from below and implementing plans from above without much autonomy" (Qian & Xu, 1993).

government and of the upper-level functional or industrial department of the central government, the former is far more influential than the latter. In a word, a fragmented structure between the central government and local governments had already existed under the centrally planned economic system, and local governments were neither "economic eunuch" nor the blind follower of the central government.

Another important institutional arrangement in rent allocation is the state ownership of auto enterprises. With the formation of the centrally planned economic system, an absolute state-owned economy was established. Besides collective enterprises (owned by township governments and villages) in rural areas, SOEs were the main form in the national economy. Large-scaled and important SOEs were put under the direct control by different industrial ministries under the State Council. Small and less important SOEs were governed by different levels of local governments, which became the main source of their revenues (Zhang & Yuan, 2008:1~11).

China established a three-level fiscal system based on the central, provincial and county-level governments under a unified supervision of the central government in 1953. In other words, a decentralized fiscal system with division of revenue and expenditure between the central and local governments was created. In 1954, it explicitly stipulated that the revenue of local governments divided into three parts: regular income, fixed ratio shared revenue and central transfers. The sources of local governments' revenue originated from taxes and profits (including depreciation) of its local SOEs besides central transfers. The expenditure was also divided between the central and local governments. The expenditure respectively included the expenditure of all the subordinated agencies of the corresponding levels of governments, investment and other expenses of their SOEs. Although the concrete tax categories changed over time, and the ownership of the SOEs changed only between the central and local governments: decentralized fiscal structure as a whole did not change essentially. The critical point is that SOEs were the focal agents of China's auto industry.

Furthermore, the two waves of decentralization reform before 1978 strengthened the local governments.① The first wave was from 1958 to 1960, and the second one started from the late 1960s. The details of these two reforms were a little bit different, but the principal measures were similar. The first and foremost, a principle of planning system mainly based on regions instead of the whole nation was adopted, and a great extent of decision-making authority for capital investment was delegated to local governments from the central government. Supervision authority of many SOEs was delegated from the ministries of the central government to provinces and cities or even counties. A revenue sharing scheme was

① About the details of the two waves of decentralization reform, see Qian & Weingast (1996) and Wu (2004:47~48).

fixed and local governments gained some authority over taxes. In addition, enterprises were entrusted with some authority of governing personnel except some managerial and technical staffs. In this new institutional setting, the local governments were empowered with some authorities that had belonged exclusively to the central government before, such as the authority of planning, enterprise governing, material distribution, and even investment examination and approval authority, and part of the financial power and levying taxes.

Local governments were not just cogs of the huge "central planning" machine. Instead, they were given some initiatives for developing their regions and became the semi-independent economic bodies with their own interests. In this context, so many local auto-related enterprises were built during the waves of decentralization reform. The direct reason for local governments to build and keep their own auto related enterprises was that the profits coming from auto enterprises were to fall directly to the local governments.

3.4 Rent-seeking

3.4.1 Local Governments as the Principal Rent-seekers

When making the development plan for the auto industry at first, in order to meet the needs of development of national economy and military mobility, the central government attempted to build large-scale state-owned auto enterprises under its direct control. When FAW started in 1953, a second large-scale auto plant, Second Auto Works (SAW), with a double capacity during the late period of the first FYP (1953~1957) was also being prepared and a preparatory group for it was quickly set up.① Then a third large-scale auto plant was put on the agenda even when the SAW was being prepared in the mid-1960s.②

In order to make sure that the limited resources could be put into the selected SOEs, the central government issued a strict administrative regulation for the project approval in 1952.③ It stipulated that the central government itself should approve all the projects, including basic construction projects and technical transformation projects, above the limited amount. The limited amount for the auto industry is RMB 300 million, and the approving authority for auto projects between RMB 200 thousand to RMB 300 million is in the hand of FMMB.④ Considering the huge investment for auto projects, almost all the new auto-related factories should be approved by the central government or FMMB. In other words, the auto industry was protected by strict barrier to entry by the central government.

---

① This scheme was reiterated in the government work report of 1955 by the Vice Premier Li Fuchun.

② A great deal of preparatory work had been done in the mid-1970s, although this plant did not come into being.

③ In 1952, the Finance and Economy Committee of State Council issued a regulation titled "Provisional Regulation on Basic Construction Projects".

④ Here the Old RMB is converted into new currency.

Despite such a strict regulation, the result was beyond expectation. The auto industry as a whole ended up with fragmented production structure and low production capability. By the end of 1978, the number of auto plants increased to 55, producing various types of trucks, buses, and special utility vehicles, and there were 173 special purpose vehicle factories (See Figure 4). Although the reasons for such bad results are complicated, rent-seeking by the local governments is an important responsible factor to explain it. As mentioned above, the kind of rents was in the form of surplus bound to all kinds of resources. The local governments knew well that if they built their own enterprises and kept the managerial authority in their own hand, they could obtain more resources of these kinds. Thus, they wished to obtain a greater share of these rents, by inviting in their own jurisdiction more auto enterprises that were supposed to be built and financed with national capital but to benefit mainly to the local units. This activity exactly constitutes the typical rent-seeking model. The difference is that the principal actors of rent-seeking activity in China's auto industry were not entrepreneurs, firms nor interest groups but governments (local, mainly) themselves.

One clear aspect of rent-seeking in the auto industry is how local governments avoid the strict regulation of project approval by the central government to build auto enterprises (See Table 5). Before 1958, almost all of the investments in the auto industry were done by central government. From 1958, the investment by local governments increased. In the period from

1958 to 1963, the share of local governments' investment even exceeded a half, and from 1963 to 1965, the share of local governments' investment was close to a half. By the end of 1978, the accumulated investment by the local governments amounted to RMB 1.18 billion, which accounted for 24% of the total investment RMB 4.88 billion (China automotive industry yearbook, 1983:186~187).

Table 5 Central and Local Investment in the Auto Industry

1949~1978(RMB Billion)

Years	1949	1953	1958	1963	1966~1970	1971~1975	1976	1977	1978
Investment	-52	-57	-62	-65	70	75	—	—	—
Total investment (T)	0.02	0.66	0.20	0.19	0.84	1.94	0.36	0.32	0.35
Central investment (C)	0.02	0.66	0.09	0.10	0.61	1.57	0.23	0.20	0.22
Local investment (L)	0	0.09	0.11	0.09	0.23	0.37	0.13	0.12	0.13
L/T (%)	0	0	55.0	47.3	27.4	19.1	36.1	37.5	37.1

Source: China Automotive Industry Yearbook, 1983:186~187.

On the other hand, the periods of more central investment were coincident with the periods when FAW, Sichuan Auto Works, Shaanxi Auto Works and SAW were built. Only these 4 of the 55 auto plants were directly built by the central government. Most of the auto plants, the special purpose vehicle plants, and auto-parts plants were built by local governments and basically run by SOEs lacking any of entrepreneurial spirit. These auto plants in small-scale with low technology and a wrong motive could not make good use of economies of scale. It resulted in a huge waste of scarce capitals that was so short in this stage and hampered the efficiency in auto industry.

Local governments not only built auto plants, auto-related enterprises by themselves but also struggled to avoid the takeover of their enterprises by the central government from time to time. For example, in the process of concentrating auto structure by the CNAIC in 1964, local governments exerted to retain the control of their own auto related enterprises by all means.① The initial purpose of building CNAIC was to integrate all the principal auto plants and auto-parts factories scattered in different ministries and locals into one big corporation as a trust. By the end of 1963, there were more than 300 auto-parts enterprises (including motorcycle-components enterprises). Almost all of them were under the charge of local governments except that 97 factories were under direct control of MOT. At last, CNAIC took over 49 auto-parts factories from MOT, a little more than a half. On the contrary, it only took over a few auto-parts factories from the local governments. Many local auto related enterprises, such as 55 enterprises in Shanghai, including the finished auto plant Shanghai Auto Factory, were not taken over because of the strong power of Shanghai Municipal Government. When CNAIC planned to take over other local auto-parts enterprises, many local governments changed the names of their auto-parts enterprises into repair shops or special purpose factories by inquiring the information on the takeover in advance. The result was that CNAIC only took over 11

① About the details of this case, See Chen, 2003.

factories from local governments when the total number of local auto related enterprises exceeded 300. This aspect constitutes the rent-protection activity by local governments, which is a special form of rent-seeking by resisting to transferring the previously acquired rents to the other agent such as the central government.

3.4.2 State-owned Enterprises Became Rent-seekers with the Help of Local Governments

The rents in the first stage were mainly in the form of a price gap between the lower planned prices and the higher market prices. Any enterprise would benefit once it obtained investment, foreign exchange, and materials supply permission from the governing authority of auto industry. Recognizing this point, the state made two different institutional arrangements. The first one is the state ownership. There were only two kinds of enterprises: SOEs and collective enterprises (owned by township governments and villages). The SOEs were classified into two categories according to their importance and size: central SOEs, large and important, governed directly by different industrial ministries under the State Council; and local SOEs, small and less important, governed by different levels of local governments (Zhang & Yuan, 2008:1~11). Due to the nature of the auto industry, almost all the auto related enterprises were SOEs, central or local.

The second one was an accounting system of unified revenue and unified appropriation, which was enforced in all the SOEs to make sure they loyally follow the state's direction. Under such circumstances, all materials used by SOEs were supplied by the government through planning, and all their output were sold to the state, which then allocated them according to plan. All revenue was remitted to the state. SOEs remitted not only profits but also depreciation to the state, both of which were included in the government revenues. Investment in basic construction, funds for renovating fixed assets and for technological upgrading, expenses for pre-production tests, and funds for miscellaneous capital acquisition were all appropriated in fixed amounts by the departments of finance in government. The seasonal and temporal capital beyond the pre-approved amount was provided by the bank. Both workers' recruitment and their wages were arranged by the state according to plan (Lin *et al.*, 2003:55). In a word, the SOEs, central or local, would be only a kind of manufacturing shop without any decision power and managerial autonomy. In this sense, rent-seeking activities by enterprises under the centrally planned economy were uncommon. If there was any, rent-seeking of enterprises were only intended to expand their business (Lin *et al.*, 2003:211).

However, there is always an exception to every rule. Some small-size auto enterprises, with the help of local governments, became rent-seekers. During the two waves of administrative decentralization, especially the second one started from the late 1960s, quite a few state-owned auto factories, even FAW, were degraded as local enterprises, and many small-sized auto plants and auto parts factories were built by the local governments. In the two years of 1971 and 1972, the number of auto plants reached the highest record of over 100, and one province (Jiangxi) even had 14 auto plants (Liu, 2003:12). Because Culture Revolution (1966-1976) crippled central plan system, input allocations to some small SOEs were not secure. Some small enterprises were outside the central planning scope, so they could not get raw materials and other resources within the plan from the beginning. Therefore, horizontal cooperation emerged between these enterprises and different regions with the help of local governments. The small auto enterprise exchanged their auto products for raw materials by barter trading in a semi-legal black market (Liu, 2003:13). "Semi-legal" means that those exchanges were supported by local governments, but did not obtain a formal approval from the central government. Thus a dual price system, the planned price, and the black market price, emerged.① Many of the small-sized auto enterprises survived under the dual price system. In this situation, auto enterprises without sustainability to secure profits for themselves had become rent-seekers searching for the support of the local governments.

① This dual-track price system was an officially legalized form of the dual price system before 1978 (Qian and Xu, 1993).

Ⅳ. Rent Utilization in China's Auto Industry: After Reform

4.1 The Development of Auto Industry in the Transitional Economy of After Reform Stage

China did not recognize that its auto industry lagged far behind the world until witnessing dramatic import surges in sedans in the early 1980s (See Figure 9). The central government enforced a strict import restriction and imposed high tariffs on imported cars,[①] and recognized that the auto industry should be rebuilt in a more efficient way of "specialization, mass production, and economies of scale" after a long-time discussion.

① On 1st May 1981, the State Planning Commission (SPC), the State Economic Commission (SEC) and the State Machine-Building Commission (SMBC) jointly released the first provisional regulation to control the import of motor vehicles, especially sedans.

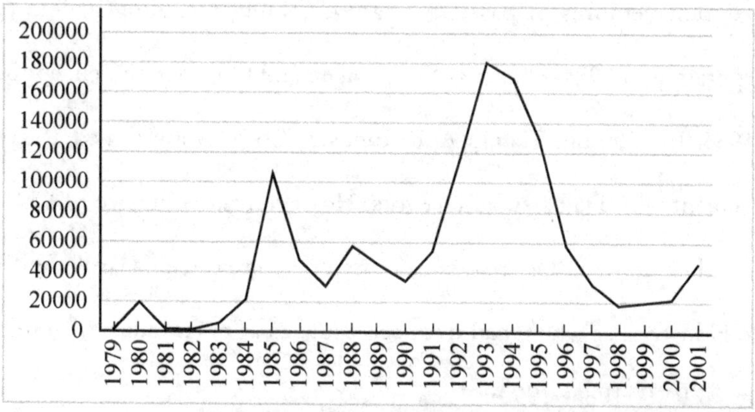

Figure 8 Imports of sedans, 1979~2001

Under this guideline, CNAIC was re-established as a dependent corporation with responsibilities of planning auto production according to national goals, and modernizing management and production processes.① Pushed by CNAIC, the truck sector as a whole developed relatively well and could roughly meet the domestic needs. In contrast, passenger car sector lagged far behind both in output and technology. So a different way of building joint ventures with foreign automakers was introduced to the passenger car sector. With the help of CNAIC,

① In May 1982, the Automobile Industry Bureau of FMMB was dissolved and the CNAIC (headed by Rao Bin) was reestablished again as a dependent corporation with the approval of State Council to meet the need of "governing economy by economic means". It became the leader of seven "associate companies (Lian Ying Gong Si)" including FAW in Changchun, SAW in Shiyan and the factories in Beijing, Tianjin, Shanghai, Ji'nan, Chongqing. FAW was renamed Jiefang, and SAW was renamed Dongfeng shortly after. However, FAW and SAW and the heavy truck plant in Ji'nan became independent from the CNAIC in 1986 but Shanghai and the other 4 ones were still under the charge of the CNAIC.

three joint ventures of passenger car were built, including Beijing Jeep Corporation in 1984, Shanghai Volkswagen and Guangzhou Peugeot both in 1985. In addition, Tianjin Auto Industry Corporation signed a license agreement with Daihatsu and Toyota. However, the influence of CNAIC was rather limited. The passenger car sector grew haphazardly and the auto industry as a whole had not been listed as a "pillar industry" until the Seventh FYP (1986~1990).

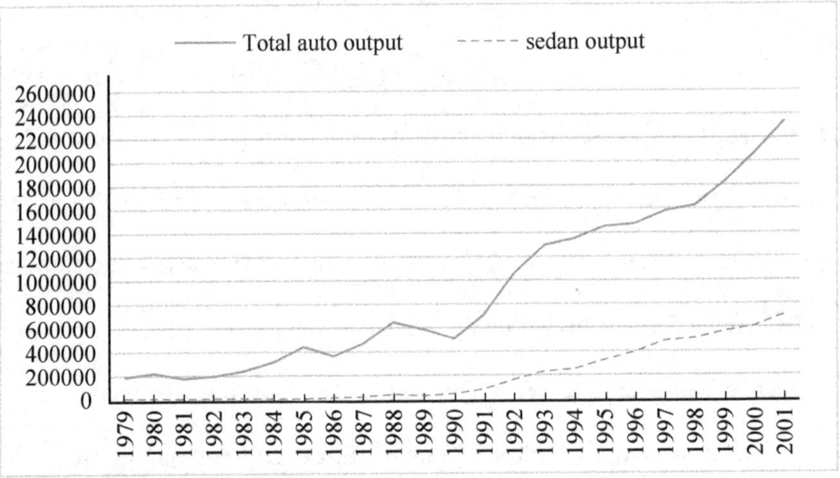

Figure 9 Output of Total Automobiles and Sedans, 1979~2001

Source: China automotive industry yearbook, 2009:46.

In order to ward off "random competition" through duplication of investment and achieving economies of scale, the central government adopted a "Large Three and Little Three" strategy in 1987 that allowed only six auto enterprises to produce passenger cars.① Subsequently,

① About the policy framework for this strategy, see details in Ngo and Chen (2009:172~173).

additional regulation for local content added in 1988. The so-called "Large Three" included the two central SOEs, FAW, and SAW, and a local state-owned Shanghai Automotive Industry Corporation (SAIC) that had built the first joint venture for sedans. Later FAW and SAW also built a joint venture. Three small auto plants, in Beijing, Tianjin and Guangzhou, the so-called "Little Three", were ratified as the auxiliary producers, because these companies had already started to engage in the production of passenger cars. The annual output of passenger cars increased year by year especially after 1990 (See Figure 10). However, the "Big Three and Little Three" strategy did not result in remarkable achievements. The number of finished auto plants kept increasing. It amounted to 124 in 1992, the most ever recorded (See Figure 10). The structure also became more fragmented in the passenger car sector. Two new auto enterprises, "Alto" and "Yunque", with the military background, broke the entry restriction to produce compact sedans.①

① In the early 1990s, China Ordnance Industry Corporation (COIC, its former was China Northern Industries Group Corporation) started its Alto mini car project under license from Suzuki. Its four plants in different provinces—Chongqing Changan, Xi'an Qinchuan, Hunan Jiangnan, Jilin Jiangbei—assembled the same model, and over 6000 Alto mini cars (compact sedans) were produced in 1991 (China Automotive Industry Yearbook, 1993:65). Guizhou Aviation Industry Corporation started to assemble a mini car named "Yunque (Subaru)" under license from Mitsubishi in 1992 (China Automotive Industry Yearbook, 1993: 62).

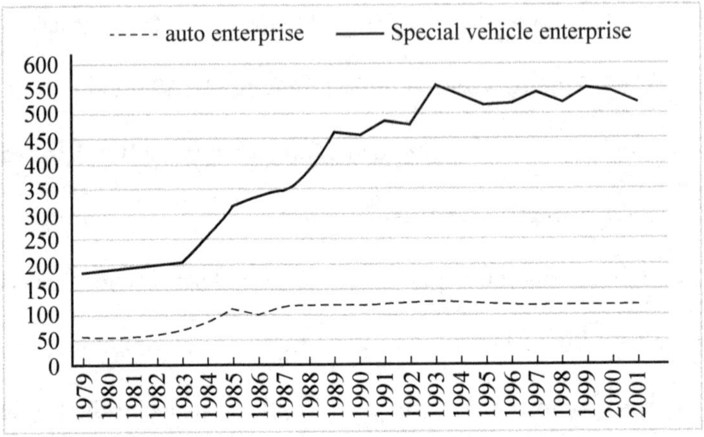

Figure 10 Number of Auto Plants, 1979~2001

Source: China Automotive Industry Yearbook, 1993:94; China Automotive Industry Yearbook, 2009:447.

In order to change this situation, Chinese government changed the governing system. The Automobile Industry Administration under Ministry of Machine-Building (MMB) was established in 1993 to exercise the day-to-day management authority. In 1994, the Auto Industrial Policy was decided and implemented.① Like the "Large Three and Little Three" strategy, the 1994 policy still used strict entry restriction as a key policy instrument, and it reiterated the 1988 regulation on local content. The implementation of the 1994 policy, however, did not achieve its goal. The industrial structure was still fragmented. Although the total number of auto enterprises in China Automotive Industry Yearbook decreased a little since 1994 (See Figure 10), in fact, the statistics of the increasing finished car enterprises was combined

① About the background to make and implement this policy, see Chin (2009: chapter 5).

into the enterprise groups (Lee, 2009). SAIC built another joint venture with GM in 1997 and many others followed in the next few years, such as Guangzhou Honda, Nanjing Fiat, and Tianjin Toyota. By the end of 2001, the enterprises of manufacturing passenger cars amounted to about 20 (China Automotive Industry Yearbook 2002: 375~376).

China's accession to WTO had brought some critical changes to the auto industry policy. The most prominent was the import restriction with tariff reduction for imported cars. As was promised in WTO accession agreement, the tariff for the finished car decreased to 25%, and the tariff for auto-parts decreased to 10% in 2006 (See Table 7). Another change was the relaxation of entry restriction. The former strict catalogue system as the main means of entry restriction was replaced by a monthly "Public Notice" system under pressure to apply for accession to WTO. "Liberalization" had appeared in the 2004 auto industry policy for the first time that allowed new auto enterprises including passenger car enterprises to be built under some required investment.①

This big relaxation brought much more foreign carmakers into China, and all the major international automakers such as Hyundai Motor, BMW, Nissan, Benz-Daimler Chrysler, had built their own joint ventures in China

① In 2004, a new "Development Policy for the Auto Industry" replaced the 1994 industry policy to strengthen the international competitiveness of China's auto industry. Although production licenses of incumbent auto enterprise were not allowed to sell, it did allow new auto enterprises, including passenger car enterprises, could be built above the required investment.

by 2006 (See Table 8). Encouraged by the success of Geely which was listed in the "public Notice" as the first private auto enterprise in 2001, many other domestic private enterprises, such as BYD, Chongqing Lifan, began to enter the passenger car sector in the following years.

Table 6 Total Automobile Output and Sedan Output 2002~2015

Year	Total output	Annual growth rate (%)	Sedan output	Annual growth rate (%)
2002	3253665	—	1092762	—
2003	4443491	36.57	2037865	86.49
2004	5070452	14.11	2312561	13.48
2005	5707688	12.57	2767722	19.68
2006	7279726	27.54	3869494	39.81
2007	8882456	22.02	4797688	23.99
2008	9345101	5.21	5037334	5.00
2009	13790994	47.57	7471194	48.32
2010	18264667	32.44	9575890	28.17
2011	18418900	8.44	14485300	51.27
2012	19271800	46.31	15523700	7.17
2013	22116800	14.76	18085200	16.50
2014	23722900	7.26	19919800	10.14
2015	24503300	3.29	21079400	5.82

Note: From 2011 to 2015, sedan output is replaced by passenger car output in this table.

Source: China automotive industry yearbook, 2011:468.

China Association of Automobile Manufacturers: http://www.caam.org.cn/

The auto industry since then has experienced explosive growth (See

Table 6). The total yearly production increased dramatically, from 3.25 million units in 2002 to 24.5 million units in 2015 when China had been No.1 in the world for years. With the sharp increase in production, the price war among auto enterprises became common after the price control over sedans was abolished in 2001. Since then auto industry has been one of the most competitive sectors. It suggests that rents in the auto industry that had existed under price control for a long time dissipated a lot.

4.2 Rents and Rent Creation

The auto industry in this stage was running under a transitional context from the centrally planned economy to a market-oriented economy after the policy of reform and opening up to the outside world officially launched in 1978. After recognizing the backwardness, China consciously imitated Japan and South Korea to implement an industrial policy to promote the development of auto industry especially the passenger car sector from the mid-1980s onwards (Eun & Lee, 2002; Huang, 2002). Import restriction, entry restriction, financial supporting besides price control were the key policy instruments that were employed by the central government to govern the development of auto industry, as in many other sectors. With the industrial policy in place, substantial rents, and rent-like transfers were created intentionally or unintentionally. This made the auto industry a lucrative business for a long time.

Rent Utilization in China's Auto Industry

The average profit of China's auto industry in the mid-1990 was reported to be 30%-60% while the profit of international auto industry was merely reported to be around 10% at the same period (Li & Tian, 1998:68). The profit for Guangzhou Honda was reported to be 22% compared to 3% for Honda globally, the profit for Shanghai VW was reported to be 15% compared to 2% for VW globally, and the profit of Shanghai GM in 2000 was reported to be 16% compared to 6% for GM globally. Even after China's accession to WTO when the import tariff decreased to a relatively low level, China was still the most profitable market for many automakers with the protected policy in place. It was reported that the profit of Dongfeng-Citroen was 12.2% for 2002, three times as high as the the profit of its counterpart in Europe (Machintosh & Mcgregor, 2003:15). The auto industry in China still had an average profit rate of 8.1% for 2003, far higher than the international level. In the same year, Nissan had a profit rate of 6.5%, Ford 2.4%, GM 1.9% and VW merely 1.9% (He, 2005:90).

In order to capture huge rents in the auto industry created by the central government, local governments, especially the provincial and municipal governments, also created different types of rents for their own auto enterprises in their jurisdictions. Namely, they sought to capture rents created in the central-level, by creating rents in the local-level. These activities can be considered as rent-seeking by the local governments. So this will be discussed in the rent-seeking part.

Ⅳ. Rent Utilization in China's Auto Industry: After Reform

Firstly, substantial rents in the form of interest rates of bank loans, foreign exchange rates, and price gap in varieties of products were created by a price control policy. In the early days after market-oriented reform, the "dual-track price" system was adopted. Under this system, goods were priced according to the consumer. Consumers operating within the plan paid artificially low prices. Consumers operating outside the plan had to pay higher "negotiated price". In theory, those consumers who paid the lower price were then obligated to sell their outputs to the state at below-market price, which would have deprived them of the benefits of rents. Instead, it was the state that could finally capture the rents (Wedeman, 2003:51). However, the dual-track price system in practice was not implemented literally, because SOEs often could receive inputs at the lowered price and then sell their outputs at a higher market price. As discussed in Chapter Ⅲ, the dual-track price system had already existed in the centrally planned economy before 1978, and it was just officially legalized after the Reform (Qian & Xu 1993). Adoption of this system did decrease rents in form of surplus to some extent but it did not entirely eliminate them (Liew, 1993; Wedeman, 2003). The dual-track system had been maintained until the late 1990s. Among them, the dual-track price, interest rate, and exchange rate were the most important. Such price control policies were not for the singular auto industry but for the whole national economy as before.

For the auto industry, the interest rate was fixed differently for auto industry. The chosen auto enterprises could obtain a bank loan at a much lower interest rate. In the mid-1980s, the annual interest rate of bank loans for private business was fixed at 9.36-11.52% while the one for the auto industry in which almost all the auto-related enterprises were SEOs was only fixed at 3.6%.① A similar policy about the foreign exchange rate was also designed for the auto industry. The narrow-sense dual-track price also existed in the auto industry. Most of the input for an auto plant such as steel, iron, coal and other energy were generally under this kind of price control.

On the contrary, as a kind of shortage goods, automobile prices, especially passenger car prices under control were generally set relatively high under a seller's market during the whole 1980s and the early 1990s. The auto enterprises and the permitted sellers of cars could sell cars at a fixed price higher than the market price by the state before 1994. The emergence of a buyers' market for automobiles after 1994 cut the passenger car prices, but the prices were still under the strict control of state's price fixation under which the auto enterprises could only sell a car at a price in the scope of price fluctuation that the state stipulated in advance. This stipulation was not lifted until 2001. Thus, the gap between the prices of in-plan input and highly fixed output prices generated extra huge rents in the form of surplus for the

① The former data comes from "Report of People' Bank of China on adjustment of partial interest rate of deposit and loan (1985)" , and the latter come from "Interim provisions on changing all the capital construction investment in national budgets from appropriations to bank loans (1984)" .

chosen auto enterprises

Secondly, import restrictions and high tariff created a great many rents in the auto industry. The early 1980s experienced an import surges in passenger cars and small trucks (see Figure 9), the pressure on foreign exchange and trade balance made the central government carry out strict import restrictions.① A series of concrete measures were implemented, such as import permits, import quotas control over import categories, control of foreign trade licenses and Foreign exchange. The annual quantity and types of motor vehicles had to obtain approval from the State Council. In addition, only six authorized ports in Dalian, Tianjin, Shanghai, Huangpu, Manzhouli and Huanggang were given clearance to whole-vehicle imports. This was restated in the 1994 auto policy (Ngo, 2008; Ngo &Chen, 2010).

Meanwhile, a high tariff was imposed on imported automobiles, especially passenger cars (See Table 7). The import tariff for the finished automobiles was 120%-150% and that for auto parts was 60% before 1985, but an 80% import adjustment tax was added in 1985. From 1986, the import adjustment tax was merged into the import tariff. The import tariff

① On 1 May 1981, the State Planning Commission (SPC), the State Economic Commission (SEC) and the State Machine-Building Commission (SMBC) jointly released the first provisional regulation to control the import of motor vehicles, especially sedans. On 15 October 1985, the State Council issued a notice to enforce control over the import of motor vehicles. On 31 October 1987, the State Council issued another notice to further control sedans import. An import quota system for automobiles was implemented.

for the finished automobiles with an engine displacement less than 3.0 liter amounted to 180% and the tariff for those with no less than 3.0 liter was 220%. This high import tariff kept unchanged until 1994. From then on it began to be lowered, but the whole tariff for automobiles had remained at a level above 70% before China' accession to WTO in 2001. Since then the tariff for finished automobiles had dramatically dropped to 25%, and that for auto parts to 10%, as China promised in the WTO accession agreement.

Table 7 Tariffs for Imported Automobiles, 1986~2006

Date	Engine displacement	
	<3.0 liter (%)	⩾3.0 liter (%)
1986	180	220
Apr. 1 st, 1994	110	150
Apr. 1 st, 1996	100	120
Oct. 1st, 1997	80	100
Jun. 1st, 2001	70	80
Jun. 1st, 2002	43.8	50.7
Jan. 1st, 2003	38.2	43
Jan. 1st, 2004	34.2	37.6
Jan. 1st, 2005*	30	30
Jan. 1st, 2006	28	28
Jan. 1st, 2006	25	25

Note: * Import quota system for automobiles was canceled in this year

Source: Lan Chaohui, 2006.

At first, these measures were taken by the central government to keep foreign exchange and trade balances, but the initial concern shifted over time. They were considered as means to protect the so-called national "infant industry" against foreign competition. Whatever the initial motivation was, these measures continually brought huge monopoly rents to the whole domestic auto industry, especially for the passenger car sector. In addition, the high import tariffs also created "discount rent" termed by Wank (2009:80) for the particular local governments and enterprises. Import tariffs create a gap between a lower international price and a higher price created by the imposition of a tariff. Generally, the state is the legal recipient of the tariff, but discount-rent seekers are the actual recipients often by illegal means such as smuggling and official profiteering.[1]

Thirdly, monopoly rents were also created by entry restriction on passenger cars sector. In order to ward off random competition and avoid duplication of investment, entry barrier to passenger cars sector were erected through the "Large Three and Little Three" strategy and the 1994 auto industrial policy.

The so-called "Large Three and Little Three" strategy was formed in late 1980s through quite a few administrative rules and regulations by the state council to guide the development of auto industry, especially the passenger car sector. The *State Council Notice on Further Control over Sedan Import* issued in 1987 explicitly stipulated that no other locals, ministries, and firms were allowed to build final assembly auto plant except the sedan production locations with an approval of the State Council.[2] According to *State*

---

① Discount rent is the gap between pre-taxed low price and after-tax high price. For the discount rent, there is no obvious loss to consumers but costs incurred to state tax revenue is obvious (Ngo, 2008, 2009, 2010).

② See Article 3 of *State Council Notice on Further Control over Sedan Import* issued by the State Council in 1987.

Council's Notice on Strict Control of Sedan Manufacturing Locations in 1988, all regions, ministries, and enterprises must have the clearance of the State Council before they could set up car production plants. All existing sedan projects that did not have the State Council's permission was brought to an end (Ngo, 2008). Furthermore, all projects involving the production of jeeps, mini passenger cars, and super-mini passenger car had to be submitted to the SPC for approval in order to prevent the implementation of sedan projects in disguise. Local governments and central ministries were notified that they could only invest in the production of auto parts and serve as a production partner of FAW, SAW, or SAIC.[1] Through these regulations, no factories but the "Large Three and Little Three" were permitted to produce passenger cars.

This was reiterated in the 1994 *Auto Industrial Policy* as a key policy tool. Like the "Large Three and Little Three" strategy, the 1994 policy remained strict entry restriction on passenger car sector as a key policy tool. No new whole-vehicle enterprises would be approved to entry. It stipulated that only these auto enterprises or enterprise groups with independent development capability for products and technologies and some certain production capacity would be approved to build new passenger car projects

① See Article 1~4 of the *State Council's Notice on Strict Control of Sedan Manufacturing Locations* in 1988.

or to double their annual production capacity.① In other words, only large incumbent auto enterprises were given an opportunity to expand capacity.

Project approval and a catalogue management system were adopted to enforce entry restriction. The authority of project approval was entrusted to SPA with the final decision in the hand of the State Council. During the 1980s characterized by the heavy-handed intervention, auto projects exceeding RMB 30 million had to be approved by SPA, and large joint ventures or wholly foreign-owned enterprise projects in excess of RMB 200 million had to be approved by the State Council.

A catalogue system was set in 1989 and this catalogue was updated and publicized twice a year. Although the system had changed several times

① Article 10 of the 1994 policy stipulated that the auto enterprises that meet the following criteria as of the end of 1995 would get special support (1) Enterprise with annual production capacity of over 300,000 vehicles, annual sales of over 200,000 vehicles, and capital for R&D no less than 3% of the annual sales revenue, could get the support to build an annual capacity of 600,000 vehicles (2) Enterprise with annual production capacity of over 150,000 vehicles, annual sales of over 100,000 vehicles, and capital for R&D no less than 2.5% of the annual sales revenue, could get the support to build an annual capacity of 300,000 vehicles (3) Enterprise with annual production capacity of over 100,000 vehicles, annual sales of over 80,000 vehicles, and capital for R&D no less than 2% of the annual sales revenue, could get the support to build an annual capacity of 200,000 vehicles (4) Enterprise with annual production capacity of over 20,000 heavy-duty trucks, annual sales of over 15,000 vehicles, and capital for R&D no less than 2% of the annual sales revenue, could get the support to build a moderate annual capacity (5) Enterprise with annual production capacity of over 1,500 heavy-duty large and/or medium buses, annual sales of over 1,000 vehicles, and capital for R&D no less than 2% of the annual sales revenue, could get the support to build a moderate annual capacity.

over the years, the modified system was neither elastic nor transparent until 2001.① Under such a system, a list of auto enterprises and auto models were registered in the catalogue. Only the enterprises registered in the catalogue were allowed to engage in auto production, and license plate would only be issued to vehicles that were included in the catalogue (Ngo, 2008; Ngo & Chen, 2009).

Compared with the rents created by import restriction for the whole auto industry, many monopoly rents through strict entry restriction were created for the chosen passenger car makers (i.e., the "Large Three" and "Little Three"). In order to capture such monopoly rents, many enterprises invested in a great many resources to enter the passenger car sector and the "Large Three and Little Three" strategy had been broken in the following years.

Fourthly, rents in the forms of "direct subsidy" , which is termed by

---

① A "*Provisional Regulation for the Management of Enterprises and Products Catalogue for Automobiles, Civil Special Vehicles and Motorcycles*" was firstly promulgated in 1989 by China Automobile Industry Union (CAIU) and the Ministry of Public Security (MPS), later MMB (from 1994 to 1998) instead of CAIU became the agency in charge for the catalogue with MPS. From March1998, MMB was downgraded to a State Bureau under the SETC until 2001 when was changed into the China Machinery Industry Federation (CMIF) as a trade association. From January 1st 2000 on the catalogue was merely under the charge of the State Bureau of Machine Building (SBMB), MPS ceased its responsibility. From January 1 2001, it was replaced by a monthly *Public Notice of Vehicle Producers and Their Products* under pressure of China applying for WTO membership, and the SETC became the new governing body.

Ngo (2009; 2010) including tax exemption and reductions, were created by the financial supporting measures.

In the context still characterized with a capital-scarce endowment during the whole 1980s and most of the 1990s, the principal instrument that the central government could employ was market control by government regulations rather than large-scale state financing. In order to overcome the capital difficulties, China adopted a Chinese-style industry policy that used Foreign Direct Investment (FDI) as a leverage to regulate local governments and SEOs (Thun, 2004). Therefore, rents in the forms of "direct subsidy" termed by Ngo (2009; 2010) including tax exemption and reductions, as one of the key financial supporting measures, was mainly implemented to promote auto joint ventures and their Chinese parent companies. Direct subsidy implies a benefit offered by the government to groups or individuals usually in the form of a cash payment or tax reduction and fees exemption, and so on (Ngo, 2009:18, 2010:10). Unlike monopoly rents and surplus, a direct subsidy is not connected to price. There is no direct loss to consumers, but a loss in state revenue and national resources is obvious.

The first kind of tax exemption and reductions was designed for joint ventures to absorb foreign investment. During the 1980s, the business income tax rate for auto SOEs amounted to 55 percent while that for auto joint ventures was only 33 percent. Furthermore, a policy of tax exemption for first two years and a half tax reduction for the later 3 years was implemented for auto joint ventures (Wang & Zhou, 1991). From this perspective, it is not difficult to understand that all "Three Large and Little Three" except TAW chose to build joint ventures when they were lack of capital.

The second kind of tax exemption and reductions was also for auto joint ventures. From the outset of auto joint venture's establishment, local content was required by the Chinese government to improve the manufacturing capability of auto parts. However, the local content was not improved well in the early years. Later, a policy of tax exemptions and reductions were offered to the sanctioned auto firms by the central government. The 1988 State Council's notice stipulated that a differential tax-rate policy was implemented to encourage the "Large Three and Little Three" to raise the local content by restraining them from importing knocked-down kits. On 1st April 1990, General Administration of Customs (GAC), SPA and State Administration of Taxation (SAT) together issued a *Provisional Taxation Regulations for Local Content of Sedans.*

It stipulated that joint ventures that draw in the whole-car technology could have a five-year start-up time before finishing the required local content. They could import knocked-down kits at 50% of the rate of the related tariff and value-added tax in the first three years during the start-up time, but last two years should pay normal tariffs. If the local content rate reached 40%~60%, they could pay at 75% of the tariff rate and 50% of value-added tax rate; if the local content rate reached 60%~80%, they could pay at 60 percent of the tariff rate; if the local content rate reached above 80%, they could pay at 40% of the tariff rate; and the local content rate should be increased by 20% year-by-year during the period of tariff reduction. Given almost all the joint ventures starting from assembling cars with knocked-down kits, the local content policy brought a lot of rents to the particular auto joint ventures. The same differential tax-rate policy was reiterated in the 1994 industry policy.

Given the facts that the high tariff for auto parts was imposed on at 50%~80% from 1986 to 1996 and that in the start-up phase, all the passenger car joint ventures imported knocked-down kits, many rents in the form of direct subsidy were created for those joint ventures of a passenger car.

4.3 Rent Allocation

During this After Reform stage characterized by hybrid economy, the traditional planning institutional arrangements for rent allocation still played a major role in the early days, but with the emerging market force, the whole traditional planning system in the auto industry faded out. On the other hand, the fragmented authority for project approval failed to ward off "random competition" which was the primary concern of the auto industry policies in the stage.

4.3.1 The Disappearance of Traditional Rent–allocators

The market-oriented reform in this stage was characterized by a gradual change in the centrally planned system. The traditional central planning system was still playing an important role. As the planning institutional arrangements gradually faded away from the centrally planned economic system, the rent allocation structure in the auto industry became more fragmented in the early years, and then the agencies for rent allocation inherited from the centrally planned economy stepped down from the history stage forever.

Firstly, the procurement agent for auto industry gradually lost its monopolistic authority and at last disappeared. Early in this stage, resources were still mainly allocated by the planning system to the auto industry. Materials Bureau, as the procurement agent, experienced a series of changes. After the Materials Bureau was set as a State General Bureau with a high administrative rank direct under the State Council on November 1975, it was degraded to a State Common Bureau in May 1982, and then in April 1988, it was again upgraded as a ministry (Fu, 1993). At last, the Materials Ministry as an important agent of the centrally planned economy was dissolved in 1994 and stepped down from the history stage.

During this process, the local governments obtained in the early years more authority to allocate materials which had been put under the central government with the deepening of administrative decentralization reform.

For example, the Category I materials under unified allocation of the state reduced from 256 kinds in 1984 to 27 kinds in 1987 and only 5 kinds in 1998.① The enterprises began to obtain authority to sell part of their own products within the planning and all the products outside of the planning. For instance, steel, one of the most important materials used in the auto industry, was sold by the steel enterprises themselves amounted to 3.5% of the total amount in 1979, and this rate rose to 14.3% in 1985, and 43% in 1990 (Fu,1993). Since 1994 when the Materials Ministry was dissolved, most of the materials had not been allocated any more by the government, central or local. The sub-level agencies of both the central and local governments for allocating materials were changed into independent trade companies. Since then it was the market force that played the main role as an allocation means in the economy.

Secondly, the authority of distributing finished automobiles was also not in the hand of the materials governing agencies under the central government any more. In the early 1980s, the authority of distributing auto productions became fragmented. The CNAIC was rebuilt in 1982 and established its own company, China Automobile Industry Sale and Service Company (CAISSC) for sale of auto-parts. Thus, CNAIC obtained the authority to sell

① The first two number comes from Fu (1993), while the last number comes from *There are only 5 kinds of materials of mandatory plan in our country,* Guangming Daily, http://www.gmw.cn/01gmrb/1998-2/16/GB/17605%5eGM5-1606.HTM. They were crude oil, natural gas, refined oil, coal and automobile.

the finished automobiles outside the state plan while the Mechanical and Electrical Equipment Company (MEEC) under the Materials Bureau sold automobiles within the state plan.

In addition, the auto enterprises also obtained part of the authority to sell the automobiles that they produced. Due to the economic reform that transferred authority from government to enterprises, the auto enterprises were at first permitted officially by the central government to produce and sell automobiles outside the state plan.[①] Then in 1983, the auto enterprises obtained authority to sell 10% of finished trucks within the state plan with the help of the CNAIC. In 1984, the auto enterprises were permitted to sell the automobiles outside of the state plan at a price within 20% higher than the state-fixed price (Liu, 2003:14). In 1986, the central government permitted some other ministries, such as Ministry of Aerospace and Aviation and Ministry of Ordnance, to build their auto sale companies to sell finished automobiles because of their strong military background.

With the deepening of reform, the auto sale companies, such as CAISSC and MEEC and their branches, under the direct control of the central ministries, changed into independent trade companies after their governing ministries were dissolved in 1994. As a whole, automobiles allocated by the state decreased to 30% in 1987, and then to 15 % in 1992, and less than 5%

① In fact, the auto enterprises began to produce more automobiles than the state plan and exchange them for what they needed badly underground from the late 1970s. This was only a subsequent confirmation.

in 1995 (Liu, 2003:14). By then the state monopolistic distribution authority existed no longer.

Thirdly, the governing authority of manufacturing agent changed frequently in the changeable context of the transitional political economy and the governing agency was ultimately dissolved. As the governing authority of manufacturing agents, the FMMB changed into Ministry of Machine Building (MMB) in 1982. During the whole 1980s, the rebuilt CNAIC[①] under MMB and its successor China Automobile Industry Union (CAIU) were responsible for the day-to-day management of auto industry. CNAIC insisted on large-scale production and Soviet-style central control, but it did not have adequate authority to push the auto industrial development. It had an ambivalent status within the bureaucratic hierarchy with conflicts with the MMB; its budget is tight; its director did not see eye to eye with the central leadership; it received only little profit from automobile sales and its subordinate associate companies (Ngo & Chen, 2009).

The CNAIC existed only for 5 years and was changed into "China

① On May 1982, the Automobile Industry Bureau of FMMB was dissolved and the CNAIC (headed by Rao Bin) was reestablished again as a dependent corporation with the approval of State Council to meet the need of "governing economy by economic means". It became the leader of seven "associate companies (Lian Ying Gong Si)" including FAW in Changchun, SAW in Shiyan and the factories in Beijing, Tianjin, Shanghai, Ji'nan, and Chongqing. FAW was renamed Jiefang, and SAW was renamed Dongfeng shortly after. However, FAW and SAW and the heavy truck plant in Ji'nan became independent from the CNAIC in 1986 but Shanghai and the other 4 ones were still under the charge of the CNAIC.

Automobile Industry Union" (CAIU) in June 1987, but it kept its English name CNAIC for international trade. In fact, it lost its authority as a "Corporation" to make final policy decisions related to technology import, quality control, and domestic sales and it was entrusted with some function as a trade association to give advice for the auto industry. It was a transitional regulation organization in the process from planned economy to market economy. With the same personnel of the CNAIC and means of governing, it was similar to the former CNAIC but with less governing authority. The CAIU did not work well with a twofold function, as a governing body and as a trade association. Therefore, the CNAIC was reestablished for another time in February 1990 and later in the same year, the CAIU was changed into China Association of Automobile Manufactures (CAAM) that became a real trade association.

The CNAIC did not do well either and in October 1993 it was changed into an exclusively state-owned company just like other companies, such as FAW Group and Dongfeng Group which were independent of CNAIC in 1986.① Its governing authority was transferred to the newly built Automobile Industry Department (AID) of new MMB which was established in 1994. After four years, MMB was degraded into the State Bureau of Machine Building (SBMB) under the State Economic and Trade Commission

① However, the CNIAC did not do well and went bankrupt in 2002. At last its assets and subsidiaries were transferred to SAIC in 2004.

(SETC) in 1998 when most of the industrial ministries were dissolved in administrative reform, and the SBMB was finally dissolved in 2001. This means the governing system inherited from the traditional centrally planned economy for the auto industry came to its end.

4.3.2 The Fragmented Authority of Project Approval

The primary concern of the auto industry policies in the After Reform stage is to ward off "random competition", and so project approval was used as the most principal mechanism for rent allocation. In fact, project approval was not particularly devised for auto industry; it was enforced by the central government for the whole national economy in 1952.① The project was divided into two categories: basic construction project and technical transformation project. As a whole, the project approval was principally enforced by the planning agency itself with the State Council but was shared with the other industrial ministries and with local governments (mainly the province-leveled governments) according to the prohibitive amount of the project investment. Through the two waves of decentralization reform before 1978, local governments obtained part of this authority. As the reform went further, local governments and other agencies obtained more of this authority.

① In 1952, the Finance and Economy Committee of State Council issued a regulation titled "*Provisional Regulation on Basic Construction Projects*". It stipulated that all the projects shall be approved by the central government, including basic construction projects and technical transformation projects, above the limited amount.

From 1985, the authority went to SPC, shared with province-level governments and relevant ministries. The large and medium-sized projects and the project with total investment more than RMB 30 million should be approved by the SPC and the project with total investment over RMB 200 million should be permitted by the State Council itself. Since 1987, that criterion raised to RMB 50 million in the sectors of energy, transport and industrial raw material (State Council, 1987). The project investment less than RMB 30 million should get an approval only from province-leveled governments or the corresponding ministries of the State Council (State Council, 1984). The project with the total foreign investment over $5 million should be approved by the SPC, and the approval authority for the one below $5 million were in the hands of province-level governments and corresponding ministries of the State Council, but Tianjin Government, Shanghai Government had the authority to approve projects with total foreign investment less than $30 million, and Governments of Beijing, Liaoning, Dalian and Guangzhou could approve projects with total foreign investment less than $10 million (State Council, 1984). Later on, the amount of project invested with foreign investment less than $10 million was applied to all the province-level governments, and the investment value was increased to $30 million in 1996 (State Council, 1996).

The project approval in the auto industry was supposed to be carried out under this formally unified regulation, but in fact, the auto industry, especially the passenger car sector, underwent a much stricter control by the central government after a surge of new auto enterprises emerged in the mid-1980s. The central government issued a strict administrative regulation in 1988 to enforce the "Large Three and Little Three" strategy. It stipulated that all projects involving the production of jeeps, mini cars, and super-mini-cars had to be submitted to the SPC for approval. Such stricter regulation was issued repeatedly. In 1997, the central government reiterated that all the finished auto (including special vehicle and bus) projects and engine projects, basic construction project or technical transformation project, should get approval from the SPC through a pre-examination by the MMB. However, the auto parts projects were not included in the regulations and so the auto parts project observed just the unified regulations. "Project approval mechanism" through formal plus de facto regulations secured rents to auto segments, more rents to autos than auto parts segment. These rent allocation structure and its main tools can be summarized in Figure 11.

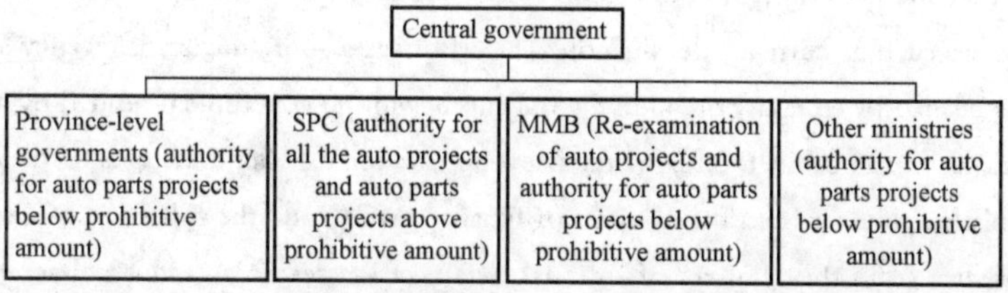

Figure 11 The Fragmented Structure and Rent Allocation Mechanism

The SPC had broad planning and administrative control over the Chinese economy and its function was similar to Economic Planning Board (EPB) in Korea.① Unlike EPB in Korea, the power of SPC was limited in fact. The SPC had the same administrative rank as other ministries of the State Council and the provincial governments. This means that it was not independent enough from other ministries and local governments. This prevented the SPC from coordinating different interests of the ministries at the central government level, to control over local governments, especially the provincial governments, which obtained some critical decision-making authority in the process of administrative decentralization. In other words, the authority of project approval also had a similarly fragmented structure as in the stage of centrally planned economy.② This structure made it easier for auto enterprises to enter into the passenger car sector with the help of local governments.

---

① EPB was created by the Park regime in the early 1960s to integrate and centralize economic decision making with the explicit purpose to reduce business influences so that the government could have a freer hand to implement politically difficult policies such as currency devaluation. The EPB was a supra-ministerial agency and it was headed by a deputy premier, the only agency in the government headed by a vice premier in the cabinet. EPB merged several economic policy functions of different ministries, budget from the Minister of Finance (MOF) and the collection of national statistics from the Ministry of Internal Affairs. EPB set up an industrial screening committee and convened regular meetings to supervise the implementation of economic policies. The members included ministers from Ministry of Commerce and Industry (MCI), MOF, and other concerned ministries (Huang, 2002).

② See Chapter Ⅲ of this book.

4.4 Rent-seeking

In this transitional economy system, the rent-seeking activities became more diverse and complicated. Much more kinds of rents were created and more different players emerged in addition to previous stage players. Therefore, the rent-seeking activities will be focused on new players other than existent ones of previous Before Reform stage. However, there will be some overlaps for overall analysis.

4.4.1 Rent-seeking by Local Governments

In this stage, with a transitional political and economic context, local governments gained more authority through further administrative decentralization and had dominant powers to push the local economic development. As in the previous stage, they were still one of the main rent-seekers but with more strength by more means.

Capturing discount rents through official profiteering and smuggling

"Discount rent" created by the high import tariff was pursued by local governments and enterprises through different means. A notorious case was the Hainan car scandal of 1984, which is identified as official profiteering by Ngo & Chen (2009). Hainan was exempted from import restriction and high import tariff to spur the development of the island by the central government, but the imported goods were only allowed to be used in its own jurisdiction. Under this policy, over 89,000 cars and other vehicles import were approved by Hainan officials and then they were resold at 3-5 times of imported prices to other areas where the tariffs exemption was not permitted (Ngo & Chen, 2009).This accrued a great many rents to the Hainan government.

As high tariff and smuggling are twins, smuggling car has never ceased since then with the high import car tariff imposed. For example, it was reported that about 100, 000 cars were smuggled through different ways, costing US$ 15 billion in 1993 (Li, 1994). Most of the big smuggling cases were done with public funds or bank loans by the SOEs with the help of local governments and/or the central government agencies.

Cracking the protection wall by building their own auto enterprises

Like in the Before Reform stage, the rent-seeking activities of the local governments in the After Reform stage were firstly manifested in building their own auto-related enterprises. It was reported that in 1985 there were 2, 904 auto firms all over the country, but only 1, 553 of them were under the charge of MMB, accounting for only 53%. The number of finished auto plants increased dramatically from 55 in 1979 to 82 in 1984 and to 114 in 1985, and the number of special vehicle factories increased from 185 in 1979 to 314 in 1985 (China Automotive Industry Yearbook, 1993:94). Despite the strict entry restriction enforced by the central government in place, the number of auto enterprises continually increased, and it reached 124 in 1992 hitting a record high. Although the total number of auto enterprises in *China Automotive Industry Yearbook* decreased a little since 1994, in fact, the statistics of the increasing finished car enterprises was combined into the enterprise group (Lee, 2009). Most of them were created directly by local governments, especially before the mid-1990s when government investment was still the main form in the auto industry and other heavy industrial sectors, or by help with local governments.

The fragmented structure of rent allocation was to blame for the far-flung production factories. As discussed above, the provincial governments and different ministries were entrusted with the authority of project approval below RMB 30 million from 1985. The strict entry restriction in place taken into consideration, a great many newly built auto firms tactfully avoided the approval of the central government. As was seen in the *State Council's Notice on Strict Control of Sedan Manufacturing Locations* issued in 1988, the central government reemphasized that all projects involving the production of jeeps, mini cars, and super-mini-cars had to be submitted to the SPC for approval in order to prevent the implementation of sedan project "in disguise". This means not a few auto enterprises were created in the mid-1980s without an approval of the central government. As the case discussed in the following, Although Chery Auto was built as a finished car enterprise from the beginning, Wuhu city government registered as "Anhui

Auto-parts Industrial Company" in disguise to tactfully avoid the central government's approval.

Helping their enterprises to enter the passenger car sector

Rent-seeking activities by local governments and central ministries were also manifested in helping the auto enterprises within their jurisdiction or under their control to enter into the passenger car sector in which the strict entry restriction was in place. Despite the "Large Three and Little Three" strategy, some enterprises managed to obtain policy exception by the strong supporting of the central ministries. As mentioned above, in the early 1990s, Guizhou Aviation Industry Corporation (GAIC) and China Ordnance Industry Corporation (COIC) entered the passenger car sector by assembling mini cars. Both COIC and GAIC were central SOEs engaging in the defense industry. The former was under the direct control of Ministry of Ordnance and the latter was under the charge of Ministry of Aerospace and Aviation. Their military background gave them strong bargaining power to lobby the central government who controlled the final say for the project approval of passenger car.

Local governments also managed to help the auto enterprises under their direct control or within their jurisdiction. Chery Auto in Wuhu was a good example.[①] Chery Auto was built directly by Wuhu municipal government. It was a joint investment by 5 SOEs subordinated to Anhui

---

① About the details of Chery Auto, See Chen (2010), Lu & Feng (2005:83~97).

Provincial government and Wuhu municipal government, and the municipal party secretary of Wuhu, Zhan Xialai, held the post of the Chairman of the board of Chery from 1997 to 2004. It was reported that Chery Auto at first was registered as "Anhui Auto-parts Industrial Company", only manufacturing engines in 1997 with a total registered capital RMB 1.752 billion. In fact, Chery Auto aimed to build as a finished car maker from the beginning in 1995 when the entry restriction for passenger car sector was strictly kept by the central government. For one thing, they began to plan and prepare the first sedan model early in 1995 when Chery Auto was listed as the "secret No.1 project of Ninth FYP in Anhui". For another, the finished car factory including stamping, welding, flame spraying and final assembly kegan to be built in 1998, the second year after it was set up officially as an engine maker. In 1999 only three years after the "auto-parts" enterprise started, the first sedan rolled down from the assembly line of Chery Auto. In the following year, about 2000 sedans were produced although Chery Auto did not obtain the production license for passenger car then yet. In order to make the newborn carmaker survive, the cars made by Chery Auto was designated as taxis in Wuhu by the provincial and municipal governments. However, this did not solve the essential problem. In order to obtain the production license, the provincial and municipal governments tried every means but failed. At last, Chery Auto in 2001 offered 20% of its shares free to SAIC in exchange for its production license. However, this was only expedient and the ties between Chery Auto and SAIC severed in 2004. Chery Auto bought back its share and has become an independent car maker with its own brand since then.

Rent-seeking through local protectionism

Prior to mid-1990s local governments often owned or had an overwhelming control over local auto enterprises, and this gave them a direct financial interest in maximizing local enterprises' profits. In addition, the auto industry that could offer high economic and tax return, afford strong economic linkage to a wide range of local auxiliary sectors, and provide plenty of employment opportunities. Therefore, local government often made every effort to help the development of their auto enterprises. Besides providing local auto enterprises with a variety of subsidies, tax reduction, fees exemption and other benefits which brought a large number of different types of rents for the picked auto enterprises, local governments also use local protectionism to protect local auto enterprises. Narrowly local protectionism refers to the erection of illicit local trade barriers and the use of discriminatory regulations to protect the local economy and local economic interests from outside competition (Wedeman, 2003:84).

Prior to the mid-1990s, most of the yearly output of the 120 finished auto firms and 400-500 special vehicle factories all over the country owned by different levels of governments were quite small. In order to help the local firms survive or develop fast, local governments often took some administrative measures to restrict autos manufactured out of their controlled enterprises to their jurisdiction. It was easy to ensure that locally produced automobiles were favored because most automobiles were bought by state or collective units during that period. For example, Shanghai Municipal Government created a taxi company in 1989 and designated Santana produced by SVW, the joint venture under its control to be the only car to be used (Wedeman, 2009). Later, the local governments often disguised the local protectionism by setting standards for the taxi in ways that discriminate against certain brands. For example, the Beijing government in the mid-1990s managed to remove many Tanjin Xiali from city roads by mandating that taxis have a minimum amount of trunk space than that of Xiali' popular models (Wedeman, 2009). This was also true in many other cities that time under similar discriminatory regulations. In this stage, local governments played as the focal actor of rent-seeking in the auto industry of China, with newly emerged enterprises and sometimes even without them.

4.4.2 Rent-seeking by Enterprises

In this stage when the Reform transferred economic authority from governments to enterprises, the great difference for rent-seeking was that the enterprises, especially the SOEs which gained some autonomy from governments began to act as another focal player of rent-seeking. In addition, the non-state owned enterprises, such as private enterprises and foreign enterprises also added as the rent-seeking players, but SOEs as a whole were still the most important players in auto as well as in other so-called "pillar" industries. Most of the time, these enterprises often conspired with local governments seeking to capture rents.

The "Large Three and Little Three" strategy—a result of rent seeking①

In this stage, due to the economic reform transferred authority from the government to enterprises, the auto enterprises became one kind of the main rent seekers. Rent-seeking activities by the auto enterprises were manifest first in the struggle for being one of the chosen enterprises of the state policy. The process of making the "Large Three and Little Three" strategy for passenger car sector was accompanied by rent-seeking activities. To some extent, this strategy per se was a result of rent-seeking.

By 1986, although the auto industry as a whole had been listed as a pillar sector, the passenger car sector did not attract special attention. The top leaders did not reach a consensus that China should develop its own passenger car sector until May 1987 when a meeting was held at Shiyan to discuss the auto industry development strategy.② At that meeting, the proposal that a new large-scale and specialized auto plants should be built in China every five years in the period of the next three Five-Year Plans

① About the details for this case, see Li (2011:41~64), Xu & Ouyang (2012:194~245), Chin (2010:77~101), Thun (2006:100~135).

② In the mid-1980s, there was a debate on whether china should produce more passenger cars. Some top-leaders disagree because considered sedans as luxury goods not means of production.

(1986~2000) by Chen Zutao, the second leader of CNAIC, was approved by the leaders in the planning agency. However, the managers of FAW and SAW, which had separated themselves from CNAIC as independent Central COEs, were strongly against that proposal. They argued that China should develop the passenger car sector based on FAW and SAW instead of building brand-new sedan plants by CNAIC. The fact was that these two central SOEs were mainly engaged in truck production. SAW had no experience at passenger car at all, and "hongqi" sedan (a model of the 1950s) project of FAW had been stopped because of its backward technology. However, these two SOEs' view was persuaded to submit to the State Council.

SAIC, as a local COE owned by Shanghai municipal government, managed to obtain the support of Rao Bin, the former head of CNAIC and FMMB who had great influence in the auto industry and top leaders. Rao Bin insisted that SAIC should be included in the proposal on the auto industry. With Rao Bin's influence, SAIC finally persuaded the top leaders to include itself in the final "Large Three", but its production capacity was limited at 30, 000 units while the other two "Large Three" were approved to establish 300, 000 unit's production capacity.

The "Little Three" that had already engaged in the production of the passenger cars as local SOEs even had no chance to attend such meetings to give their opinions. They were just ratified as the auxiliary producers because of the fait accompli. It is obvious that the enterprises selected to be the last winners were not based on outstanding performance. On the contrary, the criteria were political than economic.

The case of SAW that managed to be one of the "Big–Three" ①

In fact, SAW had no experience at making passenger cars at all ever before. In order to be listed as one of the passenger car production locations, the manager of SAW, Chen Qingtai, explored several kinds of means including sponsoring the meeting mentioned above, public lobby and private connection to the decision maker. He made good use of the mass medium to write internal reference to influence the top leaders or to directly lobby the decision makers. Before the 1987 Beidaihe meeting when the "Large Three and Little Three" strategy was made, Chen Qingtai worried whether SAW would be chosen as one of the passenger car production locations. He turned to Li Anding who was then a famous journalist working for the state media Xinhua News Agency and asked him to write an internal reference to favor SAW's export-oriented development plan for passenger cars. "Internal Reference" in Chinese reads "nei can" which refers to a kind of confidential document that published inside of the state media Xinhua News Agency only for the top leaders to read. It is an important way to influence the top leaders because it provides information and advice for them before they make critical decisions. Li managed to release the article before the starting of that meeting.

---

① About the details for this case, see Li (2011:41~64), Xu & Ouyang (2012:246~301), Thun (2006:172~206).

Chen Qingtai managed to participate in the Beidaihe meeting with the help of Bo Yongxi, the vice chairman of the board of directors of CAIU. At the meeting, Chen stated their plan directly to the top leaders. He said that SAW planned to build a passenger car plant with a production capacity of 300, 000 units in two stages. In the first stage, a production capacity of 150, 000 units would be built and the other would be built in the second stages. In addition, they planned to produce a passenger car model with an engine displacement of 1.3-1.6 liters that could not only be used as main vehicles for the official business but also could be exported to the international market. SAW's export-oriented plan was not realistic then but hit the spot because it promised to export passenger cars to earn the foreign exchange that was the most in need at that time in China. Ultimately, SAW managed to be included in the list for passenger car production base.

Forming joint ventures and, merger and acquisitions

The chosen auto enterprises according to the state policy did their best to capture the potential profits and rents immediately. The first means was to forming joint ventures with foreign automakers. All of them chose the short-cut of forming a joint venture with foreign car manufacturers. After Beijing Jeep, Shanghai VW, and Guangzhou Peugeot, FAW bought the assembly technology from Audi in 1988 and then built a joint venture with Volkswagen in 1991. SAW renamed itself Dongfeng Auto Group in 1992. To acquire the necessary technology and management know-how, it also built a joint venture with Citroen. For the chosen auto enterprises, although building a joint venture instead of developing their own technology might lead to technological dependency, it would bring them some great advantages. Firstly, it was the fastest way to produce cars to capture the monopoly rents in the protected market. Secondly, they could get tax exemption and reductions for auto joint ventures.

Moreover, another means used by central auto enterprises was merger and acquisitions. FAW and Dongfeng took the advantage of being the central SOEs to expand their reach. In a protected market, quickly expanding capacity means more rent capturing. FAW extended beyond its traditional Changchun base and set up new production plants in more than 10 provinces in the early 1990s. By 1992, it incorporated 155 auto plants, auto-parts factories, trading companies and research organizations. In a similar way, Dongfeng took over a number of smaller factories within a short period. It amalgamated about 300 firms, including many auto-parts factories (Ngo & Chen, 2009). The similar strategies were also followed by SAIC with the help of Shanghai municipal government. Many small and medium-sized factories were taken over by the large groups in the form of merger and acquisitions.

Rent–seeking by foreign automakers

Foreign automakers captured the rents created in China's highly protected auto market mainly by building joint ventures with local auto enterprises. There were three mainly three waves of building "joint ventures". The first one emerged in the mid-1980s when the SVW, Beijing Jeep, and Guangzhou Peugeot were first built and then FAW-VW, Dongfeng Citroen and the others before the mid-1995 (See Table 8).

Table 8 Joint Ventures Built in China from 1984 to 2010

Years	Joint venture	Foreign partner
1984	Beijing Jeep	AMC(Chrysler)
1985	Guangzhou Peugeot	Peugeot
1985	Shanghai VW	Volkswagen
1988	FAW-VW	Volkswagen
1993	Dongfeng Citroen	PSA Citroen
1993	Sangjiang Renault	Renault Sa
1993	Hainan Mazda	Mazda
1993	Chang' an Suzuki	Suzuki
1993	Zhengzhou Nissan	Nissan
1995	Changhe Suzuki	Suzuki
1995	Jiangling Ford(Truck)	Ford
1996	Dongwo Truck	Volvo Truck
1996	Nanjing Iveco	Iveco
1997	Shanghai GM	GM
1998	Guangzhou Honda	Honda
1999	Nanjing Fiat	Fiat
2000	(FAW)Tianjin Toyota	Toyota
2001	Chang' an Ford	Ford
2002	SAIC-GM-Wuling Auto	GM
2002	Beijing Hyundai	Hyundai

Table 8 Continued

Years	Joint venture	Foreign partner
2002	Dongfeng Yueda Kia	Kia(Hyundai)
2003	Brilliance BMW	BMW
2003	Dongfeng Honda	Honda
2003	Dongfeng Motor	Nissan
2003	Dongfeng Nissan	Nissan
2004	Guangzhou Toyota	Toyota
2005	Beijing Benz	Mercedes-Benz
2006	Chang' an Volvo	Volvo Cars
2007	Chang' an Mazda	Mazda
2007	Fujian Daimler	Daimler-Chrysler
2010	GAC Fiat	Fiat
2010	Chang' an PSA	PSA Citroen
2010	BYD-Daimler	Daimler-Chrysler
2010	Dongfeng Yulon	Yulon Motor

Source: Sun (2009), and Autoinfo (2016)

Because most of the world-top automakers could not see a promising market for passenger car, foreign automakers did not come into China in bulk. Except for SVW with a strict supervision by the Shanghai municipal government, the other two did not do well, and Guangzhou Peugeot at last exited from China in 1997 because of its poor performance. Although the reason for its exit was complicated, the rent-seeking motivation of Peugeot at first to enter China could account for a large part of the failure of

Guangzhou Peugeot.

Forming joint ventures not only made foreign auto enterprises go to local, but also allowed them to share the rents in all forms enjoyed by local partners. The Chinese government was well aware of this point and made some regulations in the 1994 industry policy. Joint ventures were required to have to carry out internal R&D, produce automobiles of international standard, and maintain foreign exchange balance. In a joint venture of assembly and engine production, foreign equity was not allowed to exceed 50%. Local content was emphasized and it was the prerequisite for permission to produce a second auto model. However, whether these requirements were actually observed was questionable. Some joint ventures did build research centers to compile with the requirement, but little genuine R&D was undertaken in the practice.

After seeing the great success of Shanghai VW, some more foreign automakers including GM, Honda, Toyota, and Fort invested large sums to China's market by forming joint ventures. This brought the second wave of building joint-ventures before China joined WTO in the end of 2001. All of the investment was not an attempt to cut cost, but "market-seeking investment" as Thun (2006:65) analyzes. Indeed, all of them jump into China's large auto market with all kinds of high rents. In the third wave from 2002 when a decreasing but still high tariff was found in China' auto market, almost all the major international large automakers came into China.

Rent–seeking by private enterprises

The main target of rent-seeking for them was to enter the highly protected auto industry especially the passenger car sector. It was much more difficult for private enterprises in the early days in the transitional context with an institutional discrimination to private ownership in the auto industry and other so-called "pillar industry" in which state ownership was the absolutely overwhelming majority before the mid-1990. However, this does not mean that the private enterprise had no chance to capture the high rents in such industries. Some private enterprises managed to enter the auto industry before 1995. In China's automotive industry yearbooks, the statistics for private auto (including motorcycle) enterprises started from 1992. The number of large and medium-sized auto (including motorcycle) related enterprises reached 10 in 1992, 19 in 1993, 44 in 1994 and 57 in 1995 respectively (China automotive industry yearbook, 1993:85; 1994:54; 1995:65; 1996:59).

From the late 1990s on, some enterprises, such as Geely, BYD and many others, even managed to enter in the passenger car sector by exploiting a policy loophole to buy production license from the incumbent auto enterprises. As mentioned above, enterprises and their car models were required to be listed in the catalogue/public notice of auto manufacturers and products before producing for the market, but the regulation did not specify that buying and selling of the license were forbidden. Enterprises especially Private enterprise used this policy loophole to crack the protection wall. Some took over existing stated-owned enterprises. For example, Geely, the first private passenger car enterprises in China, took over an auto factory at the edge of bankruptcy in 1997 (Lu & Feng, 2005:68) while BYD, used to be a famous private battery manufacturer, acquired the majority shares of a state-owned auto factory in 2003 (Zheng, 2009:62). Some others, such as Aux Group, used to be a well-known air-conditioner manufacturer, simply assembled cars under the license of Shenyang Shuangma, a light vehicle producer (Ngo & Chen, 2009).

Ⅴ. Comprehensive Analysis

This study discussed rent-seeking phenomena in China's auto industry under the plan-based economic context from a boarder perspective of rent utilization. The auto industry in china, famous for a "living fossil" of planned economy, is one of the "pillar industries" which has received great attention and intervention from the governments for a long time. Focus was given to three aspects of rent utilization: rent creation, rent allocation and rent-seeking. By examining the evolution of rent utilization in this sector, this study found out some distinguishing features in China's auto industry in the plan-based economy.

5.1 Rent Utilization in the Auto Industry

5.1.1 Rents and Rent Creation

A large number of rents of different forms exist in the whole development process of China's auto industry whatever before or after the market-oriented reform. What differs is the kind and form of rents created.

Before Reform under the centrally planned economy system, there was only one single kind of rents in the form of "surplus" (Fung, 1987; Hu, 2009) or "institutional rent" (Lin et al., 2003) created by the central government in order to build an auto sector fast with state-owned large-scale auto plants like the Soviet Union. The surplus in the form of interest rates of bank loans, foreign exchange rates, and price gap in varieties of resources that is the major one in the auto industry, were created by the low-interest-rate policy, the low-exchange-rate policy, and the low-price-control policy. Theoretically, the target beneficiary of it was the whole auto industry. After Reform in the hybrid economy, rents in the form of surplus still existed in the auto industry; this kind of rents created by the central government through the dual-track price system which was a legacy of the traditional central planned economy system for all the heavy-industrial sector including auto industry as before. This kind of rent endogenously originated from the planned economic system per se and lasted for a long time. With a deep-going market-oriented reform, it gradually decreased and at last dissipated in the auto industry in the early 2000s.

Besides, there were a few other kinds of rents After Reform. Monopoly rents were created by the central government through import restriction with a high tariff that also became "discount rent" (Wank, 2009: 80) for some particular institutions including local governments and enterprises. The initial purpose of import restriction was to maintain the balance of foreign exchange and trade, and later along with entry restriction it became a means to protect and improve the so-called "infancy industry", the auto industry, especially the passenger car sector. In addition, entry barrier erected for the passenger car sector also create many monopoly rents. Thus, monopoly rent was the most alluring in passenger car sector for a long time. As an intensified competition emerged among a large amount of automakers after China's accession to WTO due to the relaxation of import and entry restriction, monopoly rent decreased a lot.

In addition, "direct subsidy" (Ngo: 2009; 2010) in the form of tax exemption and reductions was designed for the auto joint venture by the central government. A preferential joint venture tax was designed not particularly for the auto industry, but for the whole national economy to attract foreign direct investment. The tax reduction was not abolished until 2008 when a new enterprise income tax law came into effect. The tax reduction for local contents was designed for the auto joint ventures to improve auto technology transfers which played a role of "rent for learning" (Khan & Jomo, 2000) in SVW. The accession to WTO ended it in 2001.

5.1.2 Rent Allocation

The traditional governing system of in the auto industry under the centrally planned economy, following the model of the Soviet Union, started from the mid-1950s and lasted time until the early 2000s.

FMMB, as the governing institution of auto manufacturing agents, had a fragmented authority as early as it first created. Unlike its counterpart in the Soviet Union, which took charge of all the authority of procuring, manufacturing and distributing for the whole auto industry and directly controlled over state-owned auto enterprises, FMMB only had a part authority of planning and governing production process, while the authority of procuring and distributing was scattered in different agencies in the central. Besides, there was a multilayered structure of rent allocation between the central government and local governments. In both constitutions, auto enterprises were just the production units without any autonomy.

After Reform, the rent allocation structure in the auto industry became more fragmented and meanwhile part of the authority transferred to auto enterprises in the early years. MMB lost more authority of governing auto production, while the procurement agent for auto industry gradually lost its monopolistic authority of resources allocation. Finished automobiles could be traded by diverse institutes and even auto enterprises also obtained authority to sell the automobiles that they produced. At last, the agents for rent allocation inherited from the centrally planned economy stepped down from the history stage forever. On the contrary, the project approval was used as the principal mechanism for rent allocation.

In a word, the structure of rent allocation for the auto industry was fragmented in the central and multilayered among the central-local governments from the day of its birth. From the beginning, there was a fragmented structure of rent allocation at the central level and a multilayered structure between the central government and local governments. Compared with the Soviet Union, this complicated structure could not enforce a strict control over local governments. The administrative decentralization which transferred authority from the central to local governments Before and After Reform strengthened this multilayered nature while the economic decentralization which transferred authority from governments to enterprises and families made the whole structure more fragmented, and at last the resultant force of them brought an end to it.

5.1.3 Rent-seeking

Rent-seeking activities accompany the whole development process of the auto industry, either before or after Reform. The difference is that there are different rent-seekers in the two stages.

Before Reform, rent-seeking activities by local governments emerged as a common phenomenon due to the objective existence of an "M-form hierarchical structure" which gave local governments some autonomy.[①] To obtain a greater share of the rents, local governments did not only create their own auto plants and auto related enterprises, ignoring the central government's strict regulation, but also avoided the takeover of their enterprises by the central government. The two waves of administrative decentralization strengthened the local governments and rent-seeking activities by local governments and became more widespread under the centrally planned economic system before Reform.

State-owned auto enterprises also became rent-seekers with the help of local governments despite tight control by the central government through a whole state ownership and an accounting system of unified revenue and unified appropriation. Many small state-owned auto enterprises captured rents by barter trading in a semi-legal black market.

After Reform, with a transitional political economy context, rent-seeking activities became more diverse and complicated because more kinds of rents were created by the central government and more different players emerged. Local governments gained more and more authority through further administrative

① The "M-form hierarchical structure" means that the Chinese economy is organized into a "multi-layer-multi-regional form" mainly according to territorial principle, in which each region at each layer can act as a separate operating unit. Each unit is further divided along geographic lines and at the same time controls its own enterprises along functional and specialization principle. Regions are relatively self-contained; that is, they are self-sufficient in terms of functions and supplies in production (Qian & Xu ,1993).

decentralization and became a dominant power to push the local economic development. As before, they were still one of the main kinds of rent-seekers but with more strength and by more means. Besides building auto enterprises under the direct control of them through tactfully avoiding the central government's approval as the local governments did before, they also helped auto enterprises of their own or in their jurisdiction enter the strictly protected passenger car sector. In addition, local governments also used local protectionism as a means to protect local auto enterprises from outsiders' competition. Moreover, they often provided local auto enterprises with a variety of subsidies, tax reduction, fees exemption and other benefits which brought different types of rents for the selected auto enterprises to fulfill their self-defined interest. In other words, they seek rents by creating rents.

The great difference in rent seeking from Before Reform stage was that the enterprises, especially the SOEs that gained some autonomy for the governments began to act as another main kind of rent-seekers. The target of rent-seeking for SOEs, central or local, was to become one of the picked few in the high protected passenger car sector and to quickly extend their production capacity and market share. Through all kinds of means, such as public lobby and private connection to decision maker, the most powerful state-owned auto enterprises then—FAW, SAW and SAIC—persuaded the central government to accept a so-called "Large Three and Little Three" strategy to avoid "random competition" and improve the passenger car sector in a more efficient way. Then all of the "Large Three" with many other state-owned auto enterprises chose to form joint ventures to quickly increase the market share. They also took their advantage to extend their reach by merger and acquisitions to capture monopoly rents quickly. The local stated-owned auto enterprises, such as Chery, also cracked the protective wall and entered the passenger car sector under the aegis of their local governments.

The non-state owned enterprises, such as foreign enterprises and private enterprises also started to play a great role in the rent-seeking activities. The target of rent-seeking for them was to enter the highly protected auto industry especially the passenger car sector. Foreign automakers without exception chose to form joint ventures with state-owned auto enterprises. It was much more difficult for private enterprises in the early day under the transitional context with an institutional discrimination to private ownership in the auto industry and other so-called "pillar industry" in which state ownership was the absolutely overwhelming majority before the mid-1990. Even so, some private enterprises, such as Geely and BYD managed to enter the auto industry even in the passenger car sector by exploiting a policy loophole to buy production license from the incumbent auto enterprises.

As a whole, state-owned SOEs were still the most important players in the auto industry, as in many other "pillar industries". Under most of the circumstances, these state-owned enterprises often conspired with local governments to capture rents. To some extent, it is the "tripartite alliance of rent seeking" comprised of local governments, state-owned auto enterprises and the foreign automakers that led to the failure of the auto industrial policy.

5.2 Diachronic Comparison

Based on the development of China's auto industry Before Reform and After Reform, we can summarize the major actors of rent utilization and strategies as Table 9.

Table 9 Major Actors of Rent Utilization and Their Functions and Strategies in China's Auto Industry before and after Reform

Stages	Actors	Phases	Strategies
Before Reform (in the Centrally Planned Economy)	Central Government	Rent Creation	(Low-) Price Control
		Rent allocation	Allocating rents by a fragmented structure in the central level, and a multilayered structure between central and local level
	Local Government	Rent Creation	Hard to find
		Rent allocation	Obtaining authority of raw materials and energy to their own auto enterprises in the multilayered structure between central and local level
		Rent-seeking	Avoiding tactfully the strict regulation of project approval of the central government; rent-protection by avoiding the take-over of their own auto enterprises
	State-owned Enterprise	Rent-seeking	Barter trade in a semi-legal black market
	Foreign Enterprise	Rent-seeking	Hard to find
	Private Enterprise	Rent-seeking	Hard to find

Table 9 Continued

Stages	Actors	Phases	Strategies
After Reform (in the Hybrid Economy with planning and market coexisting)	Central Government	Rent Creation	Price control, import restriction and high tariff, entry restriction, and financial supporting
		Rent allocation	Establishing a fragmented and multilayered projects approval structure
	Local Government	Rent Creation	Providing financial support, tax reduction and fees exemption to auto enterprises in their jurisdictions
		Rent allocation	Obtaining auto parts approval authority in the multilayered structure between central and local level
		Rent-seeking	Capturing "discount rents" by official profiteering and smuggling; Exploiting fragmented structure of project approval to build auto enterprises; protecting local auto enterprises from outside competition by local protectionism
	State-owned Enterprise	Rent-seeking	Providing information; public lobby; private connection to policy decision makers; building joint ventures with foreign automakers; merger and acquisitions
	Foreign Enterprise	Rent-seeking	Building joint ventures with China's incumbent auto enterprises; avoiding tactically the R&D regulations for auto joint ventures
	Private Enterprise	Rent-seeker	Exploiting policy loophole to buy production license from incumbent auto enterprises

The actors and aspects of rent utilization in the auto industry Before Reform can be also showed in Figure 12.

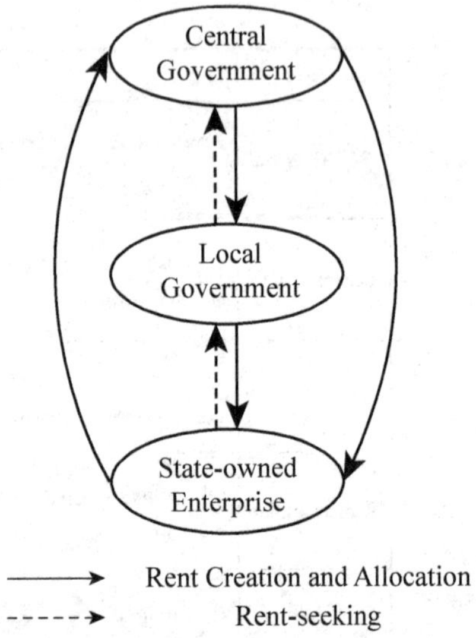

Figure 12 Rent Utilization Before Reform

The actors and aspects of the rent utilization in the auto industry After Reform can be also showed in Figure 13.

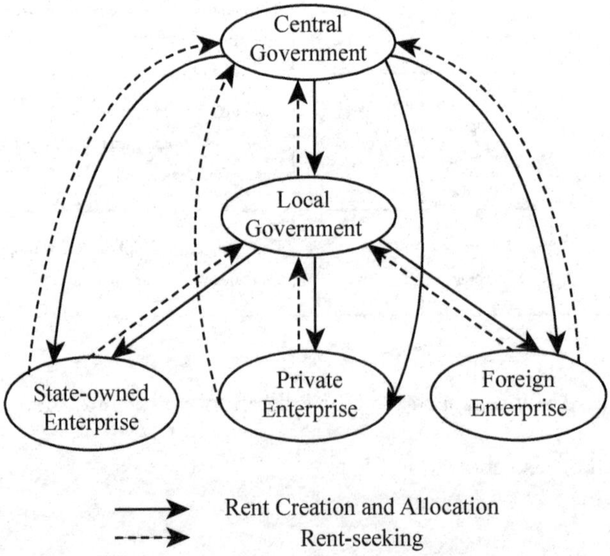

Figure 13 Rent Utilization After Reform

Ⅴ. Comprehensive Analysis

Comparison of two different stages, Before Reform and After Reform, shows some outstanding features of rent utilization in China's auto industry as follows.

Firstly, institutional rent created by central government through price control was the main sources of rent before Reform, and this type of rent endogenously originated from the planned economic system per se and lasted for a long time. With a deep-going market-oriented reform, it gradually decreased. After Reform, other types of rents were added by central and local governments through more different means.

Secondly, the structure of rent allocation for the auto industry was fragmented in the central and multi-layered among the central-local governments from the day of its birth. The administrative decentralization that transferred authority from the central to local governments before and after Reform strengthened this multi-layered nature while the economic decentralization that transferred authority from governments to enterprises and families made the whole structure more fragmented and divided, and the resultant force of them ended it in the early 2000s.

Thirdly, rent-seeking activities appeared along the whole development process of China's auto industry, whether before or after the Reform. Rent-seeking by local governments was a common phenomenon in both stages. The sharp difference between before and after Reform was that the enterprises, especially the SOEs that had gained some autonomy from the governments became another main actor of rent-seeking with many means. Besides, non-state owned enterprises, such as foreign enterprises and private enterprises also began to enter the rent-seeking game after Reform.

Fourthly, compared with the interaction between "private sector" and "government" revolving round rents and rent-seeking in the market-based economy, rent-seeking activities principally occur between State-Owned Enterprises (SOEs) and governments in China's auto industry. There is no doubt that interaction mainly occurred between governments and SOEs before Reform when a single state ownership dominated overwhelmingly the economy. With a heritage from the initial centrally planning economic system, most of the important industrial sectors, especially the so-called "pillar industries" , are still dominated by SOEs. Substantial rents created by governments, intentionally or unintentionally, principally flow into the relevant SOEs. This study found that rent exchanges in auto industry principally occur between SOEs and governments, centrally or locally, whether before or after Reform.

Fifthly, local government is a key explanatory variable in the rent utilization in China's auto industry. SOEs are generally divided into central and local SOEs according to their importance and size. On the one hand, the local SOEs that are the overwhelming majority in all SOEs are directly owned or controlled by local governments of different levels. On the other hand, all the central SOEs are always located in some regional or local areas and connected with the related local governments in different ways. In order to improve their local industrial development, local governments establish their own mechanism of rent creation and rent allocation in their own jurisdictions. The interaction revolving around rents between SOEs, local or central, and local government plays a critical role.

Sixthly, rent-seeking per se in China's auto industry can be identified as a means of destroying the monopoly of the state. In the plan-based economy, the state taking the central government as its first-level agent is the unique legitimate owner of all the rents. The central government attempted to strengthen its authority by re-centralization but failed every time. Although the ostensible target of rent-seeking by local governments and enterprises is the rents of all types created by the state, what they really attempt to change is the institutional arrangements inside the multilayered and fragmented structure of rent allocation. In other words, centrally tight control is impossible without the change of that existed multilayered and fragmented structure. Therefore, the widespread rent-seeking activities by local governments' conspiring with enterprises could be considered as one of the critical factors that push the market-oriented reform to come true.

Ⅵ. Conclusions

The auto industry in China has been the largest in the world for years. However, starting from the centrally planned economy system, it has experienced a difficult development process for the last six decades. Conventional rent-seeking literature focuses on rent-seeking activities between private enterprises and government in market economies. China's auto industry showed a complicated picture of rent utilization but had received relatively less attention. The purpose of this study is to identify the aspects of rent-utilization in China's auto industry, extending the application of the rent-seeking approach to the plan-based economic system.

The central government, local governments, SOEs are main actors in rent-utilization dynamics. The analytical model of "rent-utilization" comprising three aspects of rent-creation, rent-allocation and rent-seeking was used to extend the classical rent-seeking concept. The time frame in this study is divided into Before Reform and After Reform. Several important conclusions are drawn as follows.

Firstly, it has long been assumed in classical rent-seeking studies that government is the single unit supplying rent, but China's auto industry shows a different story. Multiple institutional and market actors are involved in the process of rent-seeking. The central government creates and allocates rents intentionally to fulfill its development strategy, and local governments do seek the rents as well as creating and/or allocating them. Auto enterprises of all kinds make every effort to capture rents created by governments, central or local. Actors utilize at least one of these aspects to maximize rents. Rent-seeking in the traditional sense needs to be extended to have more aspects. A more comprehensive term of rent-utilization including rent-creation, rent-allocation, and rent-seeking rather than the single term of rent-seeking will be more persuasive.

Secondly, the classical literature on rent-seeking treats government as a unitary unit on the assumption that the interests between the central and local government are the same. The case of China's auto industry, however, shows that the local governments had different interests from the central government in three major aspects. They wanted more auto factories built in their jurisdiction, despite opposition from the central government. They mediated direct rent trades between local SOEs, which were legally forbidden by the state laws. Local governments kept their auto parts enterprises being ceded to the central government although they was called to do so based on national interest. This interests conflicts made local governments go against the central government. It is natural that two units in a single name "government" play different roles, leading one to exploit another.

Thirdly, local governments never proved to be faithful eunuch agencies to the central government for designated national interest but the critical rent-utilizers in China's auto industry. On the one hand, they created rents as they were supposed to do and this was particularly true during the period of Before Reform. On the other hand, they fervently seek rents created by the central government. Their main strategies were using the 'discount rents', exploiting the project approval processes, mobilizing the subsidies, tax favors and local protectionism etc. When local governments themselves ran into rent utilizing game in the auto industry, every discretion and authority empowered to them to secure the most efficient implementation became powerful weapons to cause the worst inefficient results. These activities were particularly evident in After Reform era.

Fourthly, what brought local government so much discretion deserves attention. In the plan-based economy, the state is an elaborate but imperfect device of creating and allocating rents. The central government created substantial rents to develop the auto industry as one of the pillar industries. It established corresponding institutional arrangements in order to attain the goal of this industrial policy. As the monopolistic owner of these rents, it allocated them to multiple local governments and to some SOEs. In the process, substantial autonomy with oversight authority was transferred to local governments. The M-form hierarchical structure, formal decentralizations, information asymmetry and geographical remoteness caused the relationship between central and local governments to form principal-agent situation. Furthermore, local governments had interests on the tax revenues coming from SOEs in their jurisdiction. All of these conditions naturally brought much discretion to local governments.

Fifthly, while rents exchange in the market economy occours mainly between private enterprises and government, it emerged between SOEs and governments in China's auto industry. "Large Two" of the central government and so many SOEs of local governments are main producers, and the formation of 'Large Three and Little Three' strategy itself is a result of rent-seeking. Among 3 steps policy hierarchies of central government, local government and SOEs, local governments exploited the central government in collusion with local SOEs. Before Reform, central governments created substantial rents in form of surplus or institutional rent by using price discrimination and allocated them to the large-sized SOEs. The small-sized SOEs didn't have enough capabilities to capture the rents by themselves, so they could also enjoy these rents by strong powerful protectionism of local governments. This was basically true even in the After Reform stage. This suggests an absence of private businesses is not a sufficient condition to abolish rent-seeking.

Sixthly, rent-utilization in China's auto industry have caused unintended effect, helping lead to market-oriented reform. China could have put whatever price levels on the inputs and outputs as necessary for the auto industrial development. The result was a comprehensive mixture of rent-seeking, either by SOEs or local governments, with legal and/or illegal strategies. Widespread fraud, black market, corruptions etc. ensued, stimulating the public demand for the reform of the existing auto industry. Disfunction of plan-based management led China gradually not to tighter control, but to the market-oriented reform in the auto industry. The plan-based economic system gave birth to fervent rent-seeking, but the rent-seeking itself, in turn, resulted in eroding of the plan-based management and moving toward market-oriented reform.

China's auto industry had been under government intervention for a long time since its birth in the centrally planned economy. The central government had created substantial rents intentionally to carry out its development strategy and industrial policy. As the monopolistic owner of these rents, the central government established corresponding institutional arrangements to allocate all different resources with rents in order to capture the rents as much as possible and to utilize them according to its self-defined goal. Furthermore, local governments relied as well on rent creation and rent allocation in their own jurisdictions to improve their local industrial development. In both cases, rent seeking is inevitable, prevailing in the process of rent creation and rent allocation. In other words, the creation, allocation, and pursuit of rents had been embedded in the regulatory framework that governs the industrial development at the national as well as the local level. To a great extent, rent utilization in China's had been institutionalized as the constitutive part of economic governance through intimately connecting to the political system. This had resulted in a huge waste of resources that would have been used in more profit-creating activities. From this sense, much more "liberation" needed to be pushed in the auto industry. In other words, a much more deep-going marketization reform should be pushed forward to achieve greater success in the auto industry as it had been proved since China's accession to WTO.

Rent-seeking in plan-based economies was out of research focus for a long time. The model of rent-utilization in this study does not reject or deny the wisdom of classical rent-seeking theory. Rather, this model complements and supports it. By elaborating the aspects of rent utilization, and by extending the actors beyond traditional concepts, the explanatory power of rent-seeking theory will be much strengthened.

This study has some limitations. data are so limited that more dynamics on the political decision-making of concerned persons are not covered enough. Unit of analysis is the overall auto industry in

China, so some microanalysis needs to be supplemented. This study is a qualitative study, and it would strengthen the validity to complement with quantitative approach.

References

[1] Autoinfo. Waves of joint venture and strength of independent brand, 2016. http://www.autoinfo.org.cn/autoinfo_cn/content/xwzx/20160602/1519015.html.

[2] Boyd, Richard. Modes of Rent-seeking and Economic Outcomes: the case of Mexico. China Public Administration Review, 2006 (4): 1~30.

[3] Boyd, Richard. Rent-seeking in China: What Can We Learn From a Comparison with Japan and Mexico [J]. China Public Administration Review, 2008 (7): 1~23.

[4] Boyd, Richard. The Chinese Mode of Rent-utilization in Comparative Perspective [M] //Ngo, Tak-Wing and Wu, Yongping. Rent-seeking in China. London: Routledge, 2009: 254~276.

[5] Buchanan, James M., Tollison, Robert D., & Tullock, Gordon. Toward a Theory of the Rent-seeking Society [M]. College Station, TX: Texas

A&M University Press, 1980.

[6] Chen, Guangzu. Guo Li, One of the Outstanding Founders of China's Auto Industry: Try to Build an Auto Trust (CNAIC) [J]. Automobiles & Parts, 2003: 14~16.

[7] Chen, Yilin. The Mode of Rent-seeking and the Rise of Homegrown Auto Industrial Enterprises [M] //Ngo, Tak-Wing. Rent-seeking and the Industrial Development in China. Beijing : The Commercial Press, 2010: 136~165.

[8] Chin, Gregory T. China's Automotive Modernization: The Party-State and Multinational Corporations [M]. Palgrave Macmillan, 2010.

[9] Chong, Chu-young. I Was Born at This Land: My Life Story [M]. Seoul: Seoul Press, 2004.

[10] Congleton, Roger D. Hillman, Arye L. Elgar Companion to the Political Economy of rent-seeking [M]. Edward Elgar, 2015.

[11] Congleton, Roger D. Hillman, Arye L. and Konrad, Kai A. 40 Years of Research on rent-seeking—I, II [M]. Heidelberg: Springer, 2008.

[12] Economic System Comparison Editorial Department. In Search of the Roots of Corruption [M]. Beijing: China Economic Publish House, 1999.

[13] Editorial Department of China' Automobile Industry Yearbook. China Automotive Industry Yearbook (1983~2011).

[14] Eun, Jong-Hak & Lee, Keun. Is an Industrial Policy Possible in China:

the Case of the Automobile Industry [J]. Journal of International and Area Studies, 2002: 1~21.

[15] Fu, Qiang. Contemporary China's Materials Circulation [M]. Contemporary China Publish House, 1993.

[16] Fung, K. K. Surplus Seeking and Rent-seeking Through Back-Door Deals in Mainland China [J]. American Journal of Economics and Sociology, 1987 (3): 299~317.

[17] Gao Jianyi. Rent-utilization in a Plan-based Economy: the Case of China's Auto Industry [J]. Review of Institution and Economics, 2016 (2).

[18] Kang, David C. Bad Loans to Good Friends: Money Politics and the Development State in South Korea [J]. International Organization, 2002: 177~207.

[19] Harwit, Eric. China's Automobile Industry: Policies, Problems, and Prospects, Armonk, NY: M. E. Sharpe, 1995.

[20] He, Yuxin. Interpretation of Dongfeng Nisson's Business Report [J]. Caijing Magazine, 2005 (8): 88~93.

[21] He, Wei. The Rent-seeking Theory and the Establishment of Market-Economic System in China [J]. Journal of Kunming Institute of Technology, 1994 (2): 33~39.

[22] Hu, Angang. China's Political and Economic History(1949—1976) [M]. Beijing: Tsinghua University Press, 2008.

[23] Hu, Heli. Estimation of the Amount of Rents in China in 1988 [M] // Economic System Comparison Editorial Department. In Search of the Roots of Corruption. Beijing: China Economic Publish House, 1999: 42~55.

[24] Hu, Xiaobo. Transition from Surplus Seeking to Rent-seeking [M] // Ngo, Tak-Wing and Wu, Yongping. Rent-seeking in China. London: Routledge, 2009: 257~275.

[25] Hu, Xiaobo. Rent-seeking and Its Transition in China [M] //Wu, Yongping and Ngo, Tak-Wing, (eds.), Rent-seeking and the Industrial Development in China, Beijing: The Commercial Press, 2010: 257~275.

[26] Huang, Yasheng. Between two Coordination Failures: Automotive Industrial Policy in China with a Comparison to Korea [J] . Review of International Political Economy, 2002: 538~573.

[27] Jia, Xinguang. The History and Current Situation of Russia's Auto Industry. 2003. http://auto.sohu.com/66/58/article210615866.shtml.

[28] Ji, Hongjiang. The Auto Industry of the Soviet Union [J] . Journal of Foreign Studies, 1985(4): 61~65.

[29] Khan, Mushtaq H. and Jomo, K. Theory and Evidence in Asia Rents, Rent-seeking and Economic Development [M] . Cambridge: Cambridge University Press, 2000.

[30] Krueger, Anne. The Political Economy of the Rent-Seeking Society [J] .

American Economic Review, 1967 (3).

[31] Lan, Chaohui. Ultimate Goal' of Tariff Comes True, but Where Would the Imported Car market Go. http://auto.sina.com.cn/news/2006-06-20/0815194492.shtml.

[32] Lee, Khan-pyo. Local Protectionism and Industrial Restructuring in China: Evidence from Automotive Industry [J]. Journal of Korea Trade, 2009 (2).

[33] Lee, Sanghack & Cheong Kiwoong. The political economy of financial structure of Korean firms [J]. Journal of Developing Areas, 2010 (43): 221~232.

[34] Li, Dabin. A Concise Economic History of the PRC (1949~1985) [M]. Changsha: Hunan People's Press, 1987.

[35] Li, Anding. A Tale of Cars in China: 30 Years, from Start to Fast Lane [M]. SDX Joint Publishing Company, 2011.

[36] Li, Chunlin & Tian, Shu. Report on Problems of China's Auto Industrial Development, Shenyang Publishing House, 1998.

[37] Liew, Leong H. Rent-seeking and the Two-track Price System in China [J]. Public Choice, 1993 (77): 359~375.

[38] Liu, Qijun. The Economic Analysis of Rent-seeking Behavior [M]. Wuhan: Huazhong University of Science and Technology Press, 2008.

[39] Lin, Yifu Justin, Cai, Fang, Li, Zhou. The China Miracle: Development Strategy and Economic Reform. Revised Edition [M]. Hong Kong:

Chinese University Press, 2003.

[40] Liu, Yuting. Review on 50-year Development of Automobile Industry [M] //China' Automobile Industry Yearbook 2003: 5~15.

[41] Lockard, Allan & Tullock, Gordon. Efficient Rent-Seeking: Chronicle of an Intellectual Quagmire, Springer, 2001.

[42] Lu, Feng & Feng, Kaidong. The Policy Choice for Developing Auto Industry with Independent Intellectual Property Rights in Our Country [M]. Beijing: Peking University Press, 2005.

[43] Mackintosh, James & McGregor, Richard. A leap over the cliff [J]. The Financial Times, 2003 (8): 13~17.

[44] Ngo, Tak-Wing and Chen, Yilin. Rent Production and Industrial Governance in the Auto Industry [M] //Ngo, Tak-Wing and Wu, Yongping (2009), Rent-seeking in China, London: Routledge, 2009: 166~191.

[45] Ngo, Tak-Wing, and Wu, Yongping. Rent-seeking in China [M]. London: Routledge, 2009.

[46] Ngo, Tak-Wing. The Politics of Rent Production [M] //Ngo, Tak-Wing and Wu, Yongping. *Rent-seeking in China*, London: Routledge, 2009: 1~21.

[47] Ngo, Tak-Wing. Rent-seeking and Economic Governance in the Structural Nexus of Corruption in China [M] //Crime, Law and Social Change, 2008 (49): 27~44.

[48] Qian, Y. and Xu, C. Why China's Economic Reforms Differ: The M-form Hierarchy and Entry/Expansion of the Non-state Sector. Centre for Economic Performance, Discussion paper, 1993 (154).

[49] Sun, Xiujie. Review on Joint Venture and Cooperative Development of China's 60- Year Auto Industry [M] //China Automotive Industry Yearbook, 2009: 19~23.

[50] Thun, Eric. Industrial Policy, Chinese-Style: FDI, Regulation, and Dreams of National Champions [J] . Journal of East Asian Studies, 2004 (4): 453~489.

[51] Thun, Eric. Changing Lanes in China-Foreign Direct Investment, Local Governments, and Auto Sector Development [M] . Cambridge University Press, 2006.

[52] Tollison, Robert D. Rent-seeking: a Survey [J] . KYKLOS, 1982 (4): 575~602.

[53] Tullock, Gordon. The Welfare Costs of Tariffs, Monopolies, and Theft [J] . Western Economic Journal, 1967 (6): 224~232.

[54] Tullock, Gordon. The Cost of Transfers [J] . Kyklos, 1971 (24): 629~643.

[55] Tullock, Gordon. Competing for Aid [J] . Public Choice, 21, 1975 (24): 41~52.

[56] Tullock, Gordon. Rent-seeking [M] . Brookfield: Edward Elgar Publishing, Incorporated, 1993.

[57] Tullock, Gordon. Rent-Seeking Society, (The Selected Works of Gordon Tullock #5) [M] . The Liberty Fund, 2005.

[58] Wan, Anpei. An Analysis of the Composition and Major Characteristics of Rents during the Economic Transition in China [M] //Economic System Comparison Editorial Department (ed.), Search of the Roots of Corruption, Beijing: China Economic Publish House, 1999: 56~97.

[59] Wang, Fangwu & Zhou, Fangsheng. Research on the Tax System and its Reform of Auto Industry [J] . Management World (Bimonthly), 1991 (2): 132~145.

[60] Wang, Shaoguang. Steadfastly Maintain Our Direction and Explore New Roads: Sixty Years of Socialist Practice in China [J] . Social Sciences in China, 2010 (31): 21~43.

[61] Wedeman, Andrew H. From Mao to Market: Rent-seeking, Local Protectionism, and Marketization in China [M] . Cambridge: Cambridge University Press, 2003.

[62] Wedeman, Andrew. Rents, Mergers, and Acquisitions in the Automotive and Beer Industries [M] //Ngo, Tak-Wing and Wu, Yongping (eds.), Rent-seeking in China. London: Routledge, 2009: 215~240.

[63] Womack, James P., Jones, Daniel T. and Roos, Daniel. The Machine That Changed the World [M] . Free Press, 2007.

[64] Wu, Jinglian. China Economic Reform [M] . Shanghai: Shanghai Far East Press, 2004.

[65] Wu, Yuanli. The regulation failure of China's automobile industry, Ph.D. dissertation [D] . Fudan University, 2004.

[66] Wu, Yongping. Local Government, rent-seeking and Industrial Policies [M] //Wu, Yongping and Ngo, Tak-Wing. Rent-seeking and the Industrial Development in China [M] . Beijing: The Commercial Press, 2010: 37~60.

[67] Wu, Yongping and Ngo, Tak-Wing. Rent-seeking and the Industrial Development in China [M] . Beijing: The Commercial Press, 2010.

[68] Xu, Bingjin & Ouyang, Min. The Wind and Cloud of China's Passenger Car [M] . Beijing: Enterprise Management Publishing House, 2012.

[69] Yan, Shuai. Study on Industrial Concentration of Automobile Industry in China [D] . Master thesis, Chongqing University, 2009.

[70] Yang, Fan. Industrial Policy and Automobile Sector [J] . Research on Automobile Sector, 2003 (7): 23~29.

[71] Yoon, Young-Jin. A Study on Government Intervention and Rent-Seeking Activities in the Process of Economic Growth in Korea [D] . Ph.D. dissertation, Seoul National University, 1991.

[72] Yu, Jing. Why an Industrial Policy Failed in China: A Political Economic Analysis of China' Auto Industrial Policy [D] . Master

Thesis, Tsinghua University, 2005.

[73] Zhang, Cheng. Study on China's Automobile Industrial Policy [D]. Master Thesis, Central University for Nationality, 2010.

[74] Zheng, Xianbing. An Introduction to Interest Rate [M]. Beijing: China Finance Press, 1991.

[75] Zheng, Xianghu. Wang Chuanfu: the Father of BYD [M]. Beijing, Central Compilation & Translation Press, 2009.